Networth for Retirement

EVERYONE DESERVES A CONFIDENT, INDEPENDENT RETIREMENT

Beth Andrews

Networth Advisors, LLC
CANONSBURG, PENNSYLVANIA

Copyright © 2016 by Beth Andrews.

All rights reserved. No part of this publication may be reproduced, distributed or transmitted in any form or by any means, including photocopying, recording, or other electronic or mechanical methods, without the prior written permission of the publisher, except in the case of brief quotations embodied in critical reviews and certain other noncommercial uses permitted by copyright law. For permission requests, write to the publisher at the address below.

Beth Andrews/Networth Advisors, LLC
125 Technology Drive, Suite 104
Canonsburg, PA 15317
www.bethandrews.info

Book layout ©2013 BookDesignTemplates.com

Ordering information:
Quantity sales. For special discounts on quantity purchases by corporations, associations and others, contact the address above.

Networth for Retirement/ Beth Andrews. —1st ed.
ISBN 978-1530123896

Networth Advisors, LLC is a registered investment advisor. Information presented is for educational purposes only and does not intend to make an offer or solicitation for the sale or purchase of any specific securities, investments, or investment strategies. Investments involve risk and, unless otherwise stated, are not guaranteed. Be sure to first consult with a qualified financial adviser and/or tax professional before implementing any strategy discussed herein. Past performance is not indicative of future performance.

Contents

A Word from the Author

This book is for people who are retiring soon or are already retired. I have dedicated my professional life to helping you take the right steps to get to and through retirement. I often meet people who are stressed about money, afraid of running out or are just confused about whether they are doing the right thing. My job is to alleviate the fear and help keep you from making mistakes that you can't recover from.

If you are looking for a hot stock tip, I am not the financial advisor for you. But if you just want to be retired and know you are doing the most efficient things with your money, please call and we can talk.

-Beth Andrews, CPA, CFP®, ChFC®

Preface

How do you see yourself in retirement? We used to associate retirement with Ma and Pa in rocking chairs on the front porch. That is just not true of today's retirees. Now that 60 is the new 40, most people see themselves leading anything but a sedentary lifestyle. They envision their golden years as finally being their time to play. They see themselves the way television depicts retired folks: active, happy people playing on the beach with their grandchildren, playing tennis, golfing or skiing.

Retirement is no longer associated with being "put out to pasture." Some people are finding their dream job late in life. Their second careers in retirement usually center on what they really wanted to do for work all along. Others love what they are doing so much they cannot bring themselves to quit. Take Bret Favre for example. He was the football player who could not "retire" (as in quit playing) and had to "unretire" twice. Remember Bob Dylan, the nasal folk icon who sang to us in 1973: "May You Stay Forever Young?" As of 2014, he was still touring and recording at the age of 73. When Rolling Stones lead singer Mick Jagger was in his 20s, he told reporters that he would rather be dead than still singing "I Can't Get No Satisfaction" at age 45. As I write this, the ageless rocker is still belting out those lyrics to packed houses around the world at age 71.

Regardless of how you visualize your retirement, I promise you it will all be better if you have an adequate supply of money. I saw a cartoon the other day that depicted a man with a jubilant expression on his face, jumping up, clicking his heels as he exited what appeared to be an office of some sort. Well-wishers stood waving their goodbyes under a banner that read, "Happy Retirement!" This was obviously the cartoon figure's last day at his place of employment. The bubble over the man's head read: "Goodbye TENSION, hello PENSION!" The cartoonist probably did not realize that his punchline was a bit out of date. Pensions? What are those? Few retire with pensions these days.

Once upon a time in America, there was something called the "three-legged stool of retirement," which was a favorite analogy for financial security during that phase of one's financial life. Leg one of this eternal tripod was the pension — a substantial portion of your erstwhile salary, guaranteed to arrive in your mailbox the rest of your life. Pensions are also called "defined benefit pension plans." Some even come with retiree health benefits built in. Companies gave these pensions to long-time, loyal employees who stayed on the job through thick and thin for 30 years or so. The reason I am writing in the past tense is that pensions are almost extinct now. If you have one, consider yourself one of the fortunate few. They are fading into history like eight-track tapes and rotary-dial telephones.

Leg two of the stool was a rock-solid, well-funded, guaranteed Social Security system to help see you through your golden years. Social Security is underfunded. Even the system's trustees are telling us that, unless changes are made, Social Security as we know it will cease to exist for the next generation of beneficiaries. At least, it can no longer be viewed as the constant feature of retirement that it once was.

Leg three of the stool, personal savings, are threatened by interest rates that are, as this is written, at an all-time low for savers. This compels those approaching retirement to take on more risk than they are comfortable with, just to keep up with inflation.

One of the main reasons I decided to write this book is that many are unaware that alternative methods exist to help you work toward your financial independence. In this book, we will explore some of them — strategies for those approaching retirement designed to balance the need for both asset preservation and productivity throughout their golden years.

If you bought this book expecting to find a list of 10 stocks that cannot lose, see me personally, and I will make sure you get a refund. We will deal with the principles of prosperity here more than the mechanics of it. The one message you will see repeated here is not how to strike it rich quick, but how to create a financial plan designed to get you to and through retirement.

In 2011, the first of the baby boom generation (those born between 1946 and 1964) turned 65. For the next 18 years, as many as 10,000 will be turning 65 every day.[1] Will they have enough to live out the rest of their lives in comfort? Or will they have to scrimp and do without and perhaps end up becoming a burden on their families? Living the former and avoiding the latter is what this book will be about — strategies and concepts with the goal of getting you there.

We will also talk about timing and how important it is to investing. Mutual funds are great for young workers who participate in their employers' 401(k)-type retirement plans, most of which are invested in mutual funds. But as the years go by, there is a natural progression from mutual fund investing to managed accounts and more secure investments. In other words, what got you to retirement is probably not going to be what gets you through retirement.

Old Investing Ideas No Longer Work

When I first began my career as a financial advisor in 1997, a trained monkey could make money in the stock market. In fact, one did! Her name was Raven, a 6-year-old chimpanzee who, in 1999, put on a show for the press by throwing darts at a list of 133 Internet companies taped to the wall. At that time, Wall Street was dizzily setting daily growth records as the stock market rode the technology wave. The dart-throwing chimp produced a 213 percent gain, outperforming most of the fully trained professional fund managers at the time. If she had been a real fund manager, her selections would have been ranked as the 22nd best in the country out of 6,000 competitors.[2]

---

[1] Pew Research Center. Dec. 29, 2010. "Baby Boomers Retire." http://www.pewre search.org/daily-number/baby-boomers-retire/. Accessed Nov. 17, 2016.

[2] Paul B. Farrell. MarketWatch. Aug. 3, 1999. "Dart-throwing chimp still making monkey of Internet funds." http://www.marketwatch.com/story/dart-

Investors who came of age in that era thought the party would never end. If the 1980s and 1990s had been two decades with the longest economic expansion in American history, what reason was there to believe that anything could stop it? On those rare occasions when the market took a little dip, that was the time to add to your position. "Get in while the getting is good," cried the hard line optimists. "Borrow the money if you have to; there's no way we can lose."

They were wrong, of course. The dot-com bubble was like the Hindenburg coming in for a landing at Lakehurst, New Jersey; it was all about to go down in flames and those aboard were blithely unaware of the disaster that awaited them. From March 11, 2000, to Oct. 9, 2002, the Nasdaq composite lost 78 percent of its value, plunging from 5046.86 to 1114.11 points. Silicon Valley overnight millionaires were fire selling their $4 million mansions and moving back in with their parents.[3]

That economic storm eventually subsided, and the economy roared back, fueled by one of the most pronounced housing booms in the nation's history. By 2005, you could drive through neighborhoods on the outskirts of American cities and hear the staccato sound of hammers putting up houses. The Federal Reserve was keeping interest rates at an all-time low. Loans were easy to obtain because the banks could not imagine property values ever going down. If you could demonstrate that you had a pulse and could fog a mirror, you could borrow the money to buy a house. The housing bubble was forming in earnest.

---

throwing-chimp-still-making-monkey-of-internet-funds. Accessed Nov. 17, 2016.

[3] Andrew Beattie. Investopedia. "Market Crashes: The Dotcom Crash." http://www. investopedia.com/features/crashes/crashes8.asp. Accessed Nov. 18, 2016.

Then mortgage-backed securities plunged, prompting significant losses for banks and other financial institutions. Big banks — banks that were deemed "too big to fail" by the government — began to declare bankruptcy in 2008. Home values plummeted. The hammers were quiet now, and foreclosure signs started popping up in front lawns like spring flowers. On Sept. 29, 2008, the Dow fell 777.68 points — the most in any single day in history and the Dow Jones industrial average, long regarded as the barometer of the economy plunged to a new low, losing half its value.

Some market analysts have called the decade of 2000-2010 the "lost decade." There was plenty of action. The market surged up and then plunged back down, ultimately leaving investors right back where they started. Too many investors continued to invest in the 21st century the same way they did in the 20th century. That is why millions of retiring Americans lost as much as half their life's savings in the 2008 market crash. It's not about how much you make, it's about how much you get to keep!

Finding Your Number

I am usually not a big fan of TV commercials. However, a commercial about retirement caught my attention the other day. I did not catch the name of the sponsor, but the centerpiece of it all was a long, yellow wall that had been placed beside a busy downtown sidewalk. As people walked by, a man interviewed them at random, asking them, "If you could get paid for doing something you really loved, what would you do?" They were invited to write their answers on the yellow wall. Some of their answers included:

- Start a book store
- Play music

- Learn to fly
- Be a teacher
- Be an art historian

The narrator then spoke into the camera and asked, "Isn't that what retirement is all about? The point of the commercial was that retirement for most people today is a time to find their passion in life and pursue it. While this book is about the financial side of retirement, the ultimate goal is to facilitate your finding and pursuing your dreams, your goals and your passions in this very special time. Make the right decisions, and the result can be an active and happy retirement. Make the wrong decisions and the opposite can occur.

I encourage you to read on with an open mind. I once attended a seminar where the speaker asked a thought-provoking question: "If what you thought you knew to be true wasn't, when would you want to know?"

"As soon as possible," I said to myself.

Are you also that way? If what you thought was true about investing or managing your wealth turned out not to be true, when would you want to know? In the following chapters, you may be introduced to ideas and concepts that may be new to you. You may see some strategies that you were not acquainted with before. Do not let that throw you. Weigh them logically and withhold bias. Sometimes the things of greatest value lie hidden in plain sight until they are pointed out to us.

CHAPTER ONE

The Retirement Stampede

"As the baby boomers like me are retiring and getting ready to retire, they will spend whatever it takes — and they're the wealthiest generation in our country — to make themselves live an enjoyable life in their retirement years."

~ David Rubenstein

Officially, baby boomers are those born between 1946 and 1964. Baby boomers began to impact the economy immediately. In the 1950s, manufacturers could barely keep up with the demand for baby products — everything from toys and teething rings to disposable diapers.

The baby boom had a ripple effect on the U.S. economy. Servicemen returning from World War II married sweethearts and started families. This meant new homes and all the appliances needed to run them. It also meant new schools, new roads, more automobiles. The impact on the economy was like a massive, steady wave that kept building on its own momentum.

As the members of this generation passed through every stage of their lives, they changed the shape of the country's economic and social landscape and set the economic pace for American life. Boomers were the buyers and sellers of cars, homes, televisions, radios, computers and appliances. They had such an appetite for whatever the country's horn of plenty could produce that they invented a new thing called the "credit card," which they would proceed to use more and more as the years passed. The words "charge it" became a permanent part of the boomer's vocabulary. Now they could take it home and pay for it later. More than any generation that had come before, they were movers and shakers, dreamers and doers.

You know you're a baby boomer when:

- You remember watching black and white television: "The Lone Ranger," "Howdy Doody" and "Dick Van Dyke."
- You used a rotary dial phone to call your first sweetheart.
- You know what Brylcreem was used for.
- You changed TV channels with a knob.
- Sean Connery will always be James Bond to you.
- You know what a "sock hop" is.
- You listened to the Jack Benny Show on the radio.
- You remember watching the Watergate hearings, and you understood what was going on.
- Your first allowance was paid to you in change.

Now, they are retiring!

Who would have thought it? The generation that gave us rock 'n' roll is now lining up for Medicare and signing up for Social Security. The very first baby boomer turned 65 on Jan. 1, 2011. The first batch of the 78 million boomers alive today is rushing headlong toward retirement like stampeding buffalo. By some estimates, as many as 10,000 are retiring each day.[4] To put that in perspective, the capacity of Heinz Field, where the Pittsburgh Steelers play professional football, is a little over 65,000. Imagine that many people across America leaving their jobs each week and stepping into the ranks of the retired. Are they prepared to live on their savings? Most surveys and studies I have read say no. Words boomers applied to "old people" in the heyday of their youth, such as "retirement" and "Social Security," are now being used in connection with them.

American Demographer Phillip Longman makes no secret about his belief that baby boomers as a class are not ready for retirement. In his research paper entitled "Why Are So Many Baby Boomers Ill-Prepared for Retirement?", he makes the point that, while boomers were great at inventing rock 'n' roll and putting human footprints on the moon, the generation that gave us the two-car garage and the credit card hasn't been so good at saving for retirement.[5] And it's true. Boomers earned more at every age of life than any other generation in history but, as a group (though it certainly doesn't apply to all of them) they couldn't wait to spend it. Their parents probably grew up in the Great Depression, but these kids pretty much had everything they wanted. As they grew older, they could afford

---

[4] Pew Research Center. Dec. 29, 2010. "Baby Boomers Retire." http://www.pewre search.org/daily-number/baby-boomers-retire/. Accessed Nov. 17, 2016.

[5] Phillip Longman. June 5, 2008. "The Economic Impact of Aging U.S. Baby Boomers." https://www.scribd.com/document/207888209/Baby-Boomer-Economic-Impact. Accessed Nov. 17, 2016.

anything their credit score would let them buy: color TVs, new cars, nice homes and gadgets of every description. This mindset fueled the economy during the postwar expansion and kept the wheels of commerce spinning even faster through the 1990s. But now retirement is staring them in the face, many of them are taking serious inventory for the first time. Once I retire, will I have enough to live on? How can I be sure?

The Three-Legged Stool

Let's cover a bit more about the three-legged stool we mentioned in the preface of this book. Leg one was supposed to be your employer-funded pension. What transpired in the American economy to alter the underpinnings of the traditional retirement picture?

You may be a baby boomer if you remember the Studebaker. It was a car that had such a futuristic design that most people thought they were ugly. The exception may have been the Avanti, which the public considered well-built and stylish. The problem is the fickle, American car-buying public just didn't purchase enough of them to keep Studebaker in business. What does all that have to do with pensions? When Studebaker closed their South Bend, Indiana, assembly plant in 1963, its pension plan was so poorly funded that Studebaker could not afford to make good on its promises. They tried to wiggle out of their agreement by creating a staggered program in which 3,600 workers who had reached the retirement age of 60 received full pension benefits, 4,000 workers aged 40–59 who had 10 years with Studebaker received lump-sum payments valued at roughly 15 percent of the actual value of their pension benefits, and the remaining 2,900 workers received no pensions at all. Needless to say, that didn't go over too well with the labor unions, and the United Auto Workers screamed bloody murder.

The now-famous NBC news special that aired Sept. 12, 1972, was the catalyst for dramatic changes in pension laws. "The Broken Promise" was an hourlong television special that showed millions of Americans the consequences of poorly funded pension plans and onerous vesting requirements. In the following years, Congress held a series of public hearings on pension issues and public support for pension reform grew significantly. The result was the Employment Retirement Income Security Act of 1974 (ERISA). Now it would be illegal to do what Studebaker did. The new laws were so demanding on pension programs that corporations started backing away from them altogether.[6]

Leg two of the three-legged stool is supposed to be Social Security. Social Security is good for many things, and we will cover it in greater detail in a subsequent chapter. It is (1) guaranteed by the federal government (which, the last time I checked, is the only entity that can legally print money), and (2) good for one's entire lifetime. What Social Security is not, however, is enough to support you in retirement unless you can pare down your lifestyle to around the national poverty level. This might be a good time to think about your true priorities and align your assets to support your personal goals.

Leg three is personal savings. In the last few decades, the responsibility for providing for retirement income has

---

[6] Roger Lowenstein. The Wall Street Journal. Oct. 1, 2013. "The Long, Sorry Tale of Pension Promises."
http://www.wsj.com/articles/SB10001424127887732330850457908
5220604114220. Accessed Nov. 18, 2016.

largely shifted away from the government and employers to individuals. On the day you retire, you snip that umbilical cord, severing yourself forever from that regular paycheck. Now, you have to rely on other income sources for your upkeep and lifestyle. If I could say what I'm about to say with a megaphone and write it in letters as big as the letters on the Hollywood sign, I would. Plainly stated, "Please, please plan ahead!" Do not imagine that the three-legged stool will support you anymore — at least not the way it did your parents' generation.

I read a clever headline the other day about the three-legged stool becoming a "pogo stick." I wouldn't go that far. OK, so pensions are for the most part gone, but they have been replaced by 401(k)s in most places. The problem with 401(k)s is that they aren't guaranteed. Once you retire, if you don't make some prudent decisions, you could end up losing much of what you saved. Just ask those who were caught with their guard down when the 2008 financial crisis hit.

What About Personal Savings?

Personal savings is a broad area. Once you have accumulated personal wealth, where do you place those assets so you (a) won't lose them and (b) can get the most out of them in retirement? In the chapters to come, we will look at all of this. In many respects, it is like putting a puzzle together; the pieces are interlocking. One piece touches another and, in some cases, they are interdependent. A move in one area of your financial life may impact another.

I remember reading an article back in the 1990s that said retiring baby boomers could expect a tremendous transfer of inherited wealth from their parents. It was supposed to be in the trillions of dollars. For the most part, that tremendous transfer of wealth hasn't materialized. Oh,

I'm sure some boomers are rendered well off by inherited fortunes, but as a class it hasn't been enough to give them a leg up when it comes to retirement support. The Federal Reserve Bank of Cleveland conducted a survey that revealed only 2 percent of the heirs surveyed had received as much as $100,000 or more — either in cash or property value. Others received far less. The article made the observation that many who had been counting on an inheritance to help them retire were disappointed. So what happened to all that money? Much of the wealth they imagined their parents would leave to them had gone to pay for expenses incurred by their parents in the later stages of life. It should serve as a stark warning to boomers that their assets could similarly be eroded without proper planning.[7]

So your retirement income will depend mostly on your personal savings and investments. That is more responsibility, true, but it is also an opportunity. Do you have a company savings plan, such as a 401(k), 403(b) or 457 plan? These plans are tax-advantaged, but they work only if you participate in them. I hope that you have contributed the maximum and taken full advantage of your employer's matching provisions. I cannot tell you how many young people I come across who aren't contributing to their 401(k) plans at work. When I ask them why, they usually have vague answers that amount to the "I don't know" shrug. We will get into this a little deeper later in this book, but if your employer offers matching funds, that's free money! Take it!

The beauty of tax-deferred savings is that you can watch what you would have paid in taxes pump up your

---

[7] Jagadeesh Gokhale and Laurence J. Kotlikoff. Federal Reserve Bank of Cleveland. Oct. 1, 2000. "The Baby Boomers' Mega-Inheritance Myth or Reality?" http://people.bu.edu/kotlikof/1001.pdf. Accessed Nov. 17, 2016.

savings/investment account even more. That same money is then able to earn interest, and, if you leave it alone to grow, the interest on the interest earns interest and so on. That's why I lump tax-deferred savings plans such as 401(k)s and IRAs into the personal savings leg of the stool. The old pension plans didn't function that way. You got what you got, and that was it.

Again, the downside to 401(k)s and the like is that they are not guaranteed. Once you stop working, if you don't make wise decisions, you could lose some of that hard-earned, diligently-saved money due to inordinate market risk. There are many places to which you can move the money to help protect it from market risk. There are possible advantages and possible disadvantages to consider with every choice we make in this regard. Take bank CDs for example. They are safe from market risk, but, with interest rates at the time of this writing at a fraction of a percent, not a popular choice. Other financial vehicles include:

- Individual retirement accounts (IRAs)
- Roth IRAs
- Keogh plans
- SEP IRAs
- Deferred annuities

In most cases with the above, your money is not taxed until you withdraw it. With a Roth IRA, the taxes are paid with the initial premium and not taxed at all when you withdraw it. The advantage of tax deferral is that when the money stays in the account, interest continues to accrue.

There are only so many places you can put money. In the following chapters, we will get into more detail on some of them.

Herd Mentality

My mental picture when naming this chapter "The Retirement Stampede" stems from watching TV as a kid and seeing herds of buffalo galloping mindlessly across the open prairie. Spooked by lightning or the report of a rifle, the herd takes off running and tramples everything in sight. It's almost as if this massive collection of frightened animals has a single mind. For no apparent reason, the entire herd suddenly stops running. They catch their breath and go back to grazing as if to say, "What was that all about?"

The 1958 Disney film documentary, "White Wilderness" immortalized the suicidal behavior of lemmings. Millions of these furry little rodents would inexplicably make a mad dash off the edge of a cliff into the sea. Another example of "herd mentality."

Herd mentality can infect humans too — especially when it comes to making investment decisions. During the initial interview with prospective clients, I like to ask questions and listen. What do they want out of life? What are their goals, wishes and intentions? What do they want their money to do for them?

When you think about it, money is no more than numbers on paper until we attach a purpose to it. Even in its cash form, it is worthless until we exchange it for something of value. When reviewing accounts during these interviews, I will sometimes ask the simple question: "Why do you have these assets parked here?" Quite often, the answer is, "I don't know."

When we approach retirement, it is essential that we make mindful decisions and avoid "herd mentality." It is critical that we understand the "why" of our financial planning strategies. There is no one-size-fits-all strategy when it comes to planning. Each one of us is unique. One recurring theme in this book is that we must fully understand why we make the financial decisions we make and understand specifically how it affects our future. Retirement is not for mindless lemmings; there are far too many cliffs around.

Most Are Unprepared

It troubles me when I read that Americans aren't saving as much money as they used to. Sixty-two percent of Americans have savings of less than $1,000. Fourteen percent have more than $10,000 in savings.[8] Ninety-seven percent of baby boomers (those born between 1946 and 1964) don't feel like they have saved enough for their retirement. One statistic has boomers crossing the threshold of retirement at the rate of 10,000 per day.[9] That's a lot of people entering retirement unprepared, don't you think?

Another thing making matters worse is that personal debt in America is at an all-time high. Would you believe the outstanding credit card debt in the U.S. now exceeds $700 billion? And the average student graduates college owing more than $30,000 in student loans? For the first time, there is more student loan debt in the country than there is credit card debt, with a total of more than $1 trillion outstanding. This has a ripple effect throughout the entire country.[10]

---

[8] Quentin Fottrell. MarketWatch. Dec. 23, 2015. "Most Americans have less than $1,000 in savings." http://www.marketwatch.com/story/most-americans-have-less-than-1000-in-savings-2015-10-06. Accessed Nov. 18, 2016.

[9] Pew Research Center. Dec. 29, 2010. "Baby Boomers Retire." http://www.pewre search.org/daily-number/baby-boomers-retire/. Accessed Nov. 17, 2016.

[10] Erin El Issa. Nerdwallet. 2015. "2015 American Household Debt Credit Card Survey." https://www.nerdwallet.com/blog/credit-card-data/average-credit-card-debt-hou sehold/. Accessed Nov. 18, 2016.

With credit scores on the decline, more than 2 million Americans who applied for mortgage loans in 2012 were rejected.[11] In 2011, more Americans filed for bankruptcy than filed for divorce.[12],[13] Those who keep track of the financial heartbeat of the country report surveys that indicate 42 percent of the population "lives from paycheck to paycheck," and 55 percent spends more than they earn.[14]

I was disturbed to see the following statistic in the "Fast Facts & Figures About Social Security, 2014" report:

Among elderly Social Security beneficiaries, 22 percent of married couples and about 47 percent of unmarried persons rely on Social Security for 90 percent or more of their income. That's flirting with the poverty line.[15]

One of the most comprehensive reports I have ever read on the state of retirement in the United States appeared in the Accounting Degree Review, a newsletter for finance and accounting students. The report, entitled "The

---

[11] Casey Bond. GOBanking Rates, Business Insider. Nov. 16, 2012. "10 Reasons You Might Get Rejected for a Mortgage." http://www.businessinsider.com/10-reasons-you-might-get-rejected-for-a-mortgage-2012-11. Accessed Nov. 18, 2016.

[12] Best Consumer Solutions Alliance. 2012. "Bankruptcy Statistics: How Many People File Bankruptcy Each Year?" http://www.bcsalliance.com/bankruptcy_state stats.html. Accessed Nov. 18, 2016.

[13] Centers for Disease Control and Prevention. National Center for Health Statistics. 2014. "National Marriage and Divorce Rate Trends." http://www.cdc.gov/nchs/ nvss/marriage_divorce_tables.htm. Accessed Nov. 18, 2016.

[14] Employee Benefit Research Institute. 2004-2014 Retirement Confidence Surveys. http://www.ebri.org/surveys/rcs/. Accessed Nov. 18, 2016.

[15] Social Security Administration. September 2014. "Fast Facts & Figures About Social Security, 2014." https://www.ssa.gov/policy/docs/chartbooks/fast_facts/2014/. Accessed Nov. 18, 2016.

Crisis in Pensions and Retirement Plans," put forth some rather startling information. Here are a few bullet points:[16]

The Savings Shortfall

- Over the next 40 years, people over 65 will account for 20 percent of the U.S. population.
- By 2050, people over 85 will be as large a percentage of the population (4.6 percent) as people over 65 were in 1930.
- Fifty percent of all American workers have less than $2,000 saved for retirement.
- Thirty-six percent of Americans don't contribute anything to retirement savings.

Fears About Social Security

- Six out of every 10 nonretirees in the United States believe the Social Security System will not be able to pay benefits when they retire.
- Thirty-five percent of Americans over 65 rely almost entirely on Social Security payments.
- Fifty-six percent of current retirees believe the government will cut their Social Security benefits.
- In 1950, each retiree's Social Security benefit was paid by 16 U.S. workers.
- In 2010, each retiree's Social Security benefit was paid by approximately 3.3 U.S. workers.
- By 2025, there will be two workers for every retiree.

---

[16] Accounting Degree Review. 2015. "The Crisis in Pensions and Retirement Plans." http://www.accounting-degree.org/retirement. Accessed Nov. 18, 2016.

- The present value of projected benefits surpasses revenues for programs such as Social Security and Medicare by $46 trillion over the next 75 years.

Taking Responsibility

If I could say one thing overall — set goals and have a plan!

SET GOALS!

One of Yogi Berra's most famous quotes is, "If you don't know where you're going you might not get there." Oddly enough, we know exactly what the old Yankee catcher meant: Have a direction in life. Know where you're heading. Don't just let life happen to you, take charge of it and direct it.

It's easy to understand why goal setting is so difficult for so many young people. Who wants to take time out from the party of youth and engage in something so unfun and stuffy as thinking about what we want to do with the rest of our lives? Fortunately, as we get older, and our sense of obligation deepens, we are able to give some serious thought about our futures. This is especially true when young people reach the point in their lives when they want to start a family. Ask someone who is successful, and who has a little gray in their hair, what they would say to their younger self if they could go back in time. I will guarantee you that the word "goals" would probably figure prominently in the conversation, along with prodding to buying stock in Microsoft and Google.

Most Americans say they don't set goals. According to Dave Kohl, professor emeritus at Virginia Tech, based on his experiences, 80 percent of Americans say they don't have goals. He says another 16 percent say they have goals, but they just don't write them down. Less than 4 percent of those he has polled say they set goals and write them down, and only one out of 100 say they set goals, write them down and review them regularly. That's regrettable, and I hope it changes for you because it has been my experience that there is a correlation between setting goals and accumulating wealth.[17]

Goals are more meaningful if you write them down, but unwritten goals are better than no goals at all. Take the world-famous author Stephen King for example. He never wrote down his goal of being a published author and earning a living by writing. He was earning $12,000 per year as a laundry worker when he mailed off dozens of manuscripts to publishers and received rejection letters each time. Then he submitted a manuscript that, in his mind, was like all those preceding it. But this time he received a check for $400,000 in the mail for his first best-seller, "Carrie," published in 1974 and later made into a movie.[18]

Having something to reach for gives us a sense of anticipation about the future. It fuels our engine of accomplishment. We enjoy living in the present more because we are going somewhere. Just the fact that you have goals could cause your lifetime wealth to increase.

Reasons to Put Goals in Writing:

- It forces you to focus on them, and crystalizes your thinking.

---

[17] Agee Smith. Sustainable Agriculture Research & Education. "Set Goals." http://www.sare.org/Learning-Center/Bulletins/Rangeland-Management-Strategies/ Text-Version/Set-Goals. Accessed Nov. 18, 2016.

[18] Lucas Reilly. Mental Floss. Oct. 17, 2013. "How Stephen King's Wife Saved 'Carrie' and Launched His Career." http://mentalfloss.com/article/53235/how-stephen-kings-wife-saved-carrie-and-launched-his-career. Accessed Nov. 18, 2016.

- It makes you accountable. If you take a list to the grocery store or hardware store, you are more likely to get all the items.
- It helps you remember them. If, at the end of the year, you look at your goals and see that you missed achieving one or two, don't worry. You can write them down again for the new year.
- It's more like a contract.

Goals Need to Be S.M.A.R.T.

If you are like most people, you envision your future — the kind of job you want; the kind of car you want to drive; the kind of house you want to live in. Obtaining those things as you imagine them usually requires dogged determination. For goals to truly motivate us toward the accumulation of wealth, they must be S.M.A.R.T.: Specific, Measurable, Attainable, Relevant and Timely. Let's take them one at a time from the perspective of accumulating wealth.

Specific: When you specify the exact thing you wish to accomplish, you have a much greater chance of accomplishing it. For example, "land a good-paying job" is not specific enough. You need to write: "Earn $50,000 per year by age 23." You could even be more specific. "Earn $50,000 per year in salary as a chemical engineer," or "earn $50,000 per year by increasing production in my territory by $300,000 in 18 months." Goals like that give you traction. General goals just spin your wheels.

Measurable: For a goal to be meaningful, it must be measurable. A physical fitness goal may be, "I want to run three miles in 20 minutes." Or, "I want to lose 10 pounds in 30 days." A wealth goal will be measurable as well. I want to accumulate $10,000 in savings in 18 months. This gives us the ability to track our progress. If we wish to accumulate $10,000 in 18 months, we will have to put aside $555.55 per month. When we measure our progress and stay on course, reaching our target dates, we have a sense of accomplishment to encourage us to the finish line.

To accumulate wealth, you may want to take other things into account. These measurable savings goals may not seem powerful at first. But if you were to start by saving $1,000 initially, then add $600 on a monthly basis, with an average yearly interest rate of 10 percent (pretty lofty, sure, but we're using it hypothetically), you would have $1,265,960 in 30 years. That's the power of measurable goals.

Attainable: In the above illustration, becoming a millionaire in 30 years is pretty impressive! But if you aren't able to save $600 per month or attain a 10 percent interest rate, it will do you no good to set such a goal. It will only discourage you. Your goal may require some effort and sacrifice, but it must be reachable (attainable). If your goals are too difficult, you won't even try. If your goals are too easy, you won't stretch. The time frame you assign to the goal must be reasonable, too. Telling yourself you want to lose 10 pounds in 10 hours is wishful thinking. Attainable goals allow you to grow in your self-worth when you accomplish them.

Realistic: This is almost the same as attainable, but with a subtle difference. To be realistic, a goal must represent an objective toward which you are both willing and able to work. No one but you can decide just how high your goal should be. But it should be both high and realistic and represent substantial personal progress when you achieve it.

Timely: Meaningful goals occupy a time frame. Without a time limit, there is no urgency. "I want to lose 10 pounds one of these days," has no sense of urgency tied to it. "I want to lose 10 pounds by June 1, of this year," gives the goal a time limit and makes it real to you. If the goal is reasonable, attainable, realistic, specific and falls within a time frame, you are motivated to work on it by degrees and achieve it. A money goal with the same powerful elements is a powerful tool toward accumulating wealth.[19]

Break Goals into Sections

When you are setting goals for yourself, break them up into sections. You won't forget them that way, and each section accomplished is a small victory, the small parts adding up to a whole. Set yearly goals, then quarterly goals and finally monthly goals.

If you have a significant other with whom your share your life, it helps to share your goals with them. Post them in a conspicuous place. Mark your achievements on a calendar. Celebrate when they are met. Make it a family affair. Review your goals periodically and make adjustments if necessary. If you have a savings goal, of for example $100 per month, and you receive a substantial increase in salary, then revisit your goal and adjust it accordingly.

Make decisions in harmony with your goals. Let's say you and your spouse are striving to pay off your automobile loans by the end of the year and to keep on track with your savings goals of $200 per month. You are invited by a group of friends to take an expensive ski vacation. You can take the trip, and you will have many cherished memories, but it will delay paying off your auto loan, and it will derail your savings plan. It's decision time. One thing about money, you can either have the things it will buy, or

---

[19] Kori Morgan. eHow.com. "Examples of High School S.M.A.R.T. Goals." http://www.ehow.com/info_12309012_examples-high-school-smart-goals.html. Accessed Nov. 18, 2016.

you can have the money, but you can't have both. Moments like these will test your determination as a goal setter. Often the sense of fulfillment and satisfaction of reaching a goal will provide the impetus for staying the course and not giving in. On the other hand, if you can sell something you don't need on eBay and work some overtime between now and then, then you can take the trip and stay on track with your goals at the same time.

Goals are magical motivators that enable you to live where you want to live, do the kind of work you want to do and enjoy both your working life and your retirement to a greater degree. They can change you for the better and allow you to become the kind of person you wish to become.

Why Don't More People Set Goals?

I believe the reason so few people set goals is that they don't "get serious" about things. Whenever I interview highly successful people and ask them how it was that they achieved their success, they will usually tell me about a point in their lives when they just decided to "get serious," about life, work, or their savings program. Apparently, nothing happens until you "get serious" about it.

It could also be that young people who aren't in the habit of setting goals don't realize how important goals can be. Young people who began setting scholastic achievement goals while in school usually come from families in which goals were emphasized. Their parents probably set goals and discussed them around the dinner table.

Are there classes in high school on how to set goals? I haven't heard of them. There should be. Most of my clients are either retired or on the threshold of retirement, but I do occasionally work with young people, and I find they get downright excited about goal setting once they see the power behind it. In the chapters to follow, we will show how saving just a small amount of money on a regular basis can put young people on the road to wealth.

CHAPTER TWO

Oh No! We're Living Longer!

"Live as if you were to die tomorrow. Learn as if you were to live forever."

~Mahatma Gandhi

A long passenger train is rolling across the country. It's one of those that requires two diesel-electric locomotives to power it. One of the engines breaks down out in the middle of nowhere. The engineer informs everyone on board that all is well. They will rely on the second engine and travel at a lower speed. A little further down the line, the second engine breaks down, and the train comes to a stop.

The engineer, ever the optimist, wants to put a positive spin on this unpleasant situation, so he goes to each car and makes the following announcement:

"Folks, I have some good news and some bad news," says the engineer. "The bad news is that both of our engines have conked out, and it looks like we will be stuck here for quite a while."

"So what's the good news," asks a passenger.

"The good news is you're not in an airplane," says the engineer.

When it comes to the life span of baby boomers, I have some good news for you. As a demographic class, you are living longer. I will give you an average here, and then tell you how complicated it is to figure it individually. As of 2013, average life expectancy is 82. But there is much more to it than that.[20]

Averages are only averages. Set one foot on fire and put the other in a bucket of ice water and on average you are comfortable. The average life expectancy of 82, for example, is figured from birth. What difference does that make? The way life expectancy tables work, the longer you live, the longer you will live. In other words, if you live to be 65, you stand a greater chance of living to 90.[21]

There are many variables. Females live longer than males. Some ethnic groups live longer than others. Japan leads the field right now. It used to be Sweden. According to data compiled by the Social Security Administration, a man reaching age 65 can expect to live, on average, until age 84. For a woman, it's 86. One out of every four 65-year-olds today will live past age 90, and one in 10 will live past 95.[22] The Social Security website,

---

[20] Social Security Administration. "Actuarial Life Table." https://www.ssa.gov /oact/STATS/table4c6.html. Accessed Nov. 18, 2016.

[21] Andrew Menachem. Miami Herald Business News. Sept. 14, 2013. "Will you outlive your savings?" http://miamibrickellchamber.com/will-you-outlive-your-savings/.

[22] Social Security Administration. "Actuarial Life Table." https://www.ssa.gov /oact/STATS/table4c6.html. Accessed Nov. 18, 2016.

www.socialsecurity.gov, has a nifty little calculator to see how long you will live. It gives you your years of life expectancy going forward and then lets you know that the actual number may vary. The disclaimer reads: "The estimates of additional life expectancy do not take into account a wide number of factors such as current health, lifestyle and family history that could increase or decrease life expectancy."

Average life expectancy in 1950 was 68. When Social Security began in 1935, life expectancy at age 65 was 12.5 more years. By 2030, it is projected to be 21.7 for women and 19.5 years for men. The 1980 U.S. Census recorded 32,194 centenarians (age over 100) whereas the 2010 census recorded 53,364. Some experts are saying that in the 22nd century, living past 100 will be commonplace. The bottom line is whether you attributed it to better medicine, better habits or improvements in the gene pool, folks are living longer these days.[23]

So What's the Bad News?

What could possibly be negative about living longer? Life is full of counter-balances, isn't it? It seems as if every blessing comes with a disclaimer, just like those pill commercials on television. "Wonder pill is wonderful and great! Side effects may include blurred vision, nausea, heart attack, stroke and death!" Boomers are blessed and plagued, all at the same time. They have higher rates of obesity, cancer and diabetes. Could it be too much of the "good life" taking its toll? Sadly, suicide numbers are up for

---

[23] Social Security Administration. 2015. "Calculators: Life Expectancy." https://www.ssa.gov /planners/lifeexpectancy.html. Accessed Nov. 18, 2016.

this generation, too. All of this could slow down the longevity, or even reverse it.[24]

From a financial planning standpoint, however, the biggest challenge facing retirees and soon-to-be retirees today is the prospect of outliving their resources. Would you believe that more people fear running out of money when they get old than they fear death? Allianz Life Insurance Company of North America conducted a poll in 2010 and surveyed 3,257 people between the ages of 44 and 75. More than 61 percent of those surveyed said they feared depleting their assets more than they feared dying. If this is truly representative of the mood of older Americans, then three out of five seniors are haunted by the horrible thought of losing independence and becoming a burden on family members.[25]

The poll found 92 percent of survey takers believed America is facing a retirement crisis, and only 36 percent felt that their retirement nest egg was sufficient to see them through their golden years. Interestingly, the poll discovered modern retirees expect their lifestyles to surpass those of their parents.

My parents, Bill and Gloria, were both born in 1940, so they came along too early to qualify as baby boomers. They both have always had a conservative disposition toward money. I can still recall my father's admonition to save 10 percent of my earnings when I got my first job. Their propensity to live a conservative lifestyle and save for retirement has served them well in the worry depart-

---

[24] America's Health Rankings. 2016. "American's Health Rankings Senior Report."
http://cdnfiles.americashealthrankings.org/SiteFiles/PressReleases/Final%20 Report-Seniors-2016-Edition.pdf. Accessed Nov. 18, 2016.

[25] Allianz Life Insurance Company of North America. June 17, 2010. "Reclaiming the Future." http://www.retirementmadesimpler.org/Library/ENT-991.pdf. Accessed Dec. 5, 2016.

ment. So why are so many modern retirees and those coming up on retirement so edgy? Several things:

Income Uncertainty: When people received the majority of their retirement income from employer-provided, defined-benefit pension plans and Social Security, it wasn't something they had to think much about. They didn't have to plan for retirement so much because it was all planned out for them. They could put life on automatic pilot. Today, however, we live in an age of personal responsibility. That three-legged stool we talked about earlier was a comfort for earlier generations, but not now.

That translates to some tough decisions about working and post-working years. Most boomers will likely have to work longer than the typical retirement age. That probably wasn't in their original plans, but necessity may dictate a longer career path than the one they staked out when they started earning a living. The good news is that if you don't have a pension from your employer, you can create a pension-like strategy for yourself.

Spending as much as a fourth of our lives in retirement means we will have to self-manage both the accumulation and the disbursement of income. Fear is a feeling, and feelings are facts, even if they are irrational fears. Those facing retirement today wonder if they will be left high and dry by their government's public and governmental retirement and health insurance systems. They do the math and worry about fewer workers available to support a growing number of beneficiaries who are living longer.

Health Care Risk: If you live to be a ripe old age, lead a healthy, fulfilling and happy life right up to the end and die in your sleep, you have nothing to worry about. But the odds are not in favor of that. According to the U.S. Department of Health and Human Services, someone turning age 65 today has almost a 70 percent chance of needing some type of long-term care services and support in their remaining years. The average length of that care is 3.7 years for women and 2.2 years for men. Twenty percent of those who need care will need it for longer than five years.[26]

The cost of long-term care depends on the type and duration of care you need, the provider you use and where you live. But here are some averages provided by the U.S. Department of Health and Human Services, compiled from 2010 census data. Services in the Pittsburgh area may be even higher.[27]

- $205 per day or $6,235 per month for a semi-private room in a nursing home
- $229 per day or $6,965 per month for a private room in a nursing home
- $3,293 per month for care in an assisted living facility (for a one-bedroom unit)
- $21 per hour for a home health aide
- $19 per hour for homemaker services
- $67 per day for services in an adult day health care center

Doesn't Medicare cover it? No. Medicare pays for a few days of "rehabilitative" care in a nursing home. It doesn't pay for long-term illnesses that require skilled care in a nursing home for patients with Alzheimer's disease or other debilitating ailments.

---

[26] U.S. Department of Health and Human Services. "How Much Care Will You Need." http://longtermcare.gov/the-basics/how-much-care-will-you-need/. Accessed Nov. 18, 2016.

[27] U.S. Department of Health and Human Services. "Costs of Care." http://longtermcare.gov/costs-how-to-pay/costs-of-care. Accessed Nov. 18, 2016.

How about Medicaid? It is true that Medicaid pays for almost half of all long-term care in America. But to qualify for Medicaid you must officially be a pauper and, if you have some assets, that's no easy trick. Besides that, once you go the Medicaid route you become a ward of the state, and your care options become severely limited. The program is funded at the federal level and administered by the states. The rules vary a bit from state to state, but they all require you to pay for it from your own assets or use private insurance first. Once that is exhausted, then you may apply for Medicaid, but you will have to meet strict minimum eligibility requirements in order to qualify.

So that leaves self-pay or long-term care (LTC) insurance. Self-pay will erode most estates in a hurry. Traditional LTC insurance is expensive to own. The older you are, the higher the premiums. It also has other drawbacks we will get to later on along with some possible solutions.

Health care concerns are among the deepest furrows in the worried retiree's brow these days.

Market Volatility: Many retirees who had all of their personal savings invested in the stock market were rightfully nervous during the 2008 market crash. An Allianz poll said 53 percent of those interviewed watched helplessly as their net worth dropped significantly during that economic disaster. Retirement programs at work, such as 401(k)s were hit hard by the crash. This did not affect younger workers as much as it did those who were nearing retirement age. Younger workers had time for the market to recover. They could recoup their losses. Older workers, on the other hand, were at the junction in their lives where this was a non-renewable resource. They couldn't recover from their losses.[28]

Inflation: Have you ever seen beach erosion? Inflation is like that. You can't see it happening, but one summer you go to your favorite beach and half of it is gone. Inflation is not roaring now the way it was in the late 1970s; they say it's "under control" at levels under 3 percent, as this book is written. That is of little comfort to retirees who worry about living costs escalating, putting yet another element of risk to their retirement funds. "Under control" is better than "out of control." If you devalue your currency a little every month, that adds up to a massive devaluation over a number of years. How long is retirement? Twenty years? Thirty years? How much will food cost 15 years from now? How much will fuel cost then? Suppose you retired a decade ago, and your living expenses were $1,000 per month. To buy the same items — food, fuel and clothing — you would need $1,329 today. If you had retired in 1968, you would need $6,225 to buy the same things today.[29]

Longevity is a good thing. Not being prepared for it is not so great. Another wrinkle in the retiree's furrowed brow.

Looking for Security

It is no wonder, then, that retirees today are taking off the rose-colored glasses and giving their futures a good,

---

[28] Allianz Life Insurance Company.of North America. January 2010. "Five Financial Personalities." https://www.allianzlife.com/~/media/files/allianz/documents/ent1093n final201511thefivefinancialpersonalities.pdf?la=en. Accessed Nov. 18, 2016.

[29] Calculations based on inflation calculator at: Dollar Times. "Inflation Calculator." http://www.dollartimes.com/inflation/inflation.php?amount=100&year=1968. Accessed Nov. 18, 2016.

honest look. You want to know where you stand even if the news is not pleasant. That way, at least, you can make adjustments.

I find it refreshing that more and more seniors are looking for guarantees instead of projections. They should be so inclined. Many seniors lost sizable chunks of their life's savings when the stock market crashed in 2008. Only then did they perceive that perhaps they had followed bad advice. Millions of Americans found themselves having to rethink their retirement. Many of them now have to work a few extra years or pare down their standard of living because their brokers' projections turned out to be bad guesses. So I don't blame them for wanting guarantees now.

CHAPTER THREE

The Accumula-
tion Phase

"I have always paid income tax. I object only when it reaches a stage when I am threatened with having nothing left for my old age — which is due to start next Tuesday or Wednesday."

~Noel Coward

N o other phenomenon in nature is quite like the metamorphosis of a butterfly. A lowly, earthbound caterpillar goes into a few weeks of hibernation and emerges as a beautiful, feather-light winged creature wearing all the colors of the rainbow. We go through similar changes in our financial lives. The three phases are:

- Accumulation
- Preservation
- Distribution

Accumulation

With the butterfly, it is during the larval (caterpillar) stage that the most feeding and growth occurs. The caterpillar sheds its skin four or more times as it grows to accommodate its rapidly expanding body. When we stride forth from the halls of our schools and universities and enter the workplace, we begin four or more decades of earning and saving (hopefully), investing (hopefully) and growing and preparing ourselves for eventual retirement.

As a financial coach, I work primarily with the 55 and over crowd, specializing in retirement income planning. But I feel duty-bound to educate young people when I can about the principles of investing and the value of saving money when they are young. I am grateful to have parents who taught me such things. In talking with young people today, I get the feeling that I was one of the fortunate few. There is a sad lack of such education in the schools.

It seems that more often than not we send our young people out into the world without a foundation in financial education. It's a little like putting them behind the wheel of a car without basic driver's training. That's one reason so many of them don't have a clue about managing money and wind up head over heels in debt before they enter adulthood.

Is personal finance over their heads? Not at all! You do not have to be a math whiz to understand the basics of saving money and dollar-cost averaging. Since these life lessons are left for our youth to discover on their own, please allow me to provide a brief overview of what a young person will need in order to start. For the sake of motivation, let's start at the end — the reason young people should save at least 10 percent of the money they make. Let's face it, most young people don't need any lessons on how to spend money. The answer is easy: Learn to live within your means.

Learning to Save

Kids are in the accumulation stage. They are on the extreme left side of the financial timeline. It's only human nature for young people not to automatically understand the value of saving. Saving for retirement? For old age? Why do that when you are bullet-proof and immortal? You can try to teach a duck to tap dance, but it probably won't work and you will just irritate the duck. From the point of view of a financial planner, the reason you should start saving while you are young, even if you have to battle human nature, is the time value of money. The time you have on your side when you are young is such an irreplaceable gift.

The Miracle of Compound Interest

Whether Albert Einstein actually called compound interest the eighth wonder of the world or not does not change the fact that how it works is amazing. Compound interest can turn a little pile of money into a big pile of money over time. The more time you have, the more miraculous compound interest becomes.

Let's start with interest. You pay interest when you borrow money, and you earn interest when you save or invest money. There are essentially two types of interest: simple interest and compound interest. Simple interest is paid on the original principal (amount deposited) only. With compound interest, the interest is earned not only on the original principal, but also on all interests earned previously. The interest earned is added to the original amount and the money is reinvested. You earn interest on the interest on the interest, ad infinitum. You will do well in life if you borrow money only at simple interest and save and invest it at compound interest.

If you place a sum of money into an account paying compound interest and resist the urge to spend it, the accumulation factor is a bit like a snowball rolling downhill. It starts slow and small but builds upon itself until, depending on how far it rolls, gets as big as a house. If you start at the top of the hill, your snowball, by the time it reaches the bottom of the hill, will be much bigger than someone's snowball if they started, let's say, in the middle of the hill. That's a good way to illustrate the fact that the earlier you start saving and investing, the more money you have in the end.

The Case of Ann and Tom

Consider the case of Ann, age 22, who starts working after graduating from college and saves $300 per month into an account earning 6 percent compound interest. By age 28, she decides to quit her job and start a family. She stops contributing $300 per month but wisely just leaves the money in the account and lets it compound. If Ann never put another single dime into the account, guess how much she would have when she turns 65. Over $675,000! Even though she only worked six years!

Remember the snowball that someone started rolling downhill in the middle of the mountain? Tom was that guy. He postponed saving money from his paycheck until he was 31 years old. Tom can still be a millionaire by the time he turns 65, but because he started three years later than when Ann stopped contributing, he will have to save almost twice as much per year to have the same $675,000 by age 65.

The Other Side of the Coin

Compound interest is a two-edged sword. If you are paying it instead of earning it, it can be a debilitating curse. Debt wears sneakers. It can creep up on you unobserved when you are young. The free-enterprise system does not discriminate. You are a prime target. If you get into debt early, you can spend your whole life paying the lender and never get free. A revolving charge account can enslave you with interest rates of 25 percent or more.

My advice? Live within your means and avoid credit cards like the plague. If you do find yourself in credit card debt, however, pick the card charging the most interest and attack it first. Select an amount you can afford and pay it every month, no matter what. Then, when you have paid one off, celebrate with the scissors. Have a card-cutting ceremony. Toast yourself and your good judgment with your favorite ice-cold beverage. If you are like the average American, you have seven credit cards on which you carry a total balance of $15,000, annually.

You can't make compound interest work for you if it is, at the same time, working equally as hard against you.

Easy to Say; Hard to Do

Knowing how difficult it is for some young people to do, I'm going to say it anyway — there is no good reason to be in debt. A possible exception may be the mortgage on your home. If I am your financial advisor, I am going to recommend that you pay cash for everything else.

"Even my cars?" Yes, even your cars.

Understand your means and live within them. To understand your means you have to calculate (a) how much money you make, and (b) your necessary expenses, such as food, clothing, shelter and transportation. Once you put the hard numbers to it and put it on paper, you have just created a budget. The rest is discipline. Find places where you can either spend less or earn more to accomplish your financial goals.

Separate wants from needs. Do you need a new car do you just want a new car? The old axiom applies here: You can't have your cake and eat it too. A basic rule of life is that you can either have the money that it takes to buy something or you can have the item itself; you just can't have both. Some have a tendency to pluck what they want from the shelves, pay for it with credit and then convince themselves it was a need. The little angel on your right shoulder says, "Designer jeans? Really?" and the little red devil on your left shoulder whispers in your ear, "Hey, jeans are clothing. Clothing is a need!" We may play that little game with ourselves, but inside we know the truth, don't we?

Have an emergency fund. Everyone should have an emergency fund. I recommend at least six months' income tucked safely away in a liquid account. Can you use a credit card in an emergency? Of course. But having an emergency fund is a wealth-building preliminary that I recommend for all my clients as a matter of course. It's too easy to leave the debt on the credit card. When it comes to money, we have a constant fight against our own human nature, which always leans toward the course of least resistance.

The reasons for an emergency fund are obvious; it covers the what-ifs of life. What if my car breaks down and I need a new transmission? What if the roof needs repairing? What if I lose my job (there's a biggie)? What if I have an accident or get sick?

Emergency money needs to be extremely liquid. Try to find an interest-bearing account (it probably won't be much interest) that allows you to write a check, or one that allows you to access the money via an ATM.

Try to have a "hands off" policy regarding your emergency fund. You know those glass cases you see occasionally in the hallways of public buildings that say, "In case of emergency break glass?" The ones where there is usually an axe or a fire hose inside? View your emergency fund like that. Don't use it for purchases, like a down payment on a new car or home. If you are tempted to go there for a nonemergency like that, it's probably a good indicator that you should postpone the purchase.

CHAPTER FOUR

The Preservation and Distribution Phase

"I have enough money to last me the rest of my life ... unless I buy something."

~ Jackie Mason

I t may irritate statisticians and sociologists when I say this, but there is really no standard or exact definition for when one generation ends, and another generation takes over. Because my parents were both born in 1940, that officially makes them members of what the label makers say is the "Silent Generation." What is that supposed to mean? They were anything but silent! My grandparents were members of "The Greatest Generation," a term coined by broadcast journalist and author Tom Brokaw to describe those who experienced both the Great Depression and World War II. There is a lot of truth in that.

Then there are the "Baby Boomers" we discussed in Chapter One. Statisticians refer to them as the "pig in the python" generation because of the way the graph looks when you chart the birth rate after World War II. It's a flat line until 1946, bulges in the 1950s, and tapers back to flat line in 1964.

Since I was born in 1965, one year after the boom generation ended, I am officially part of what has been dubbed "Generation X." To qualify for this one, you must have entered the world after the space race began but before touch-tone phones came out. To put a broader cultural point on it, Gen Xers are identified with the decade of the 1970s the same way baby boomers are identified with the 1960s. The generation after me was named "Generation Y," sometimes called "millennials" because they witnessed the turn of the 21st century.

Economic Challenges

Each generation has its own economic challenges, some of which, just like the generations, overlap. Younger adults preparing to enter today's workforce face the oncoming tide of rising student loan debt, higher thresholds to entry-level jobs, unstable government-funded social programs, disappearing pensions, reduced benefits and higher taxes. Older Americans face many of those same challenges, along with their unique blessing/curse: the good-news/bad-news prospect of increased longevity and the possibility of outliving their resources.

A Lesson from Squirrels

Just as the economic timeline of our lives dictates when we enter and how long we stay in the accumulation phase of life discussed in the previous chapter, the same is true of the next stage I call the "preservation and distribution" phase of life. These phases of our fiscal lives remind me of the way squirrels behave in the fall. I live in Eighty Four, Pennsylvania, a rural community famous for two things: its odd name, about whose origin historians can't seem to agree, and 84 Lumber, a national building supply store chain with approximately 5,000 employees and 250 stores, which was founded here in 1957. Other than that, downtown Eighty Four is the junction of two state highways, PA 519 and PA 136. My unofficial survey, taken from my living room window, puts the population of squirrels in Eighty Four way ahead of human residents, which at the census count of 2010 stood at 657.

Nature put a toggle switch of some kind in the tiny brains of squirrels, telling them to get busy when the leaves begin to turn colors. In the autumn, I see them from my window, skittering across the lawn, gathering what I suppose are acorns and perhaps other nuts. They move frenetically, as if they were in a panic. What they are doing, of course, is stockpiling food for the winter. They instinctively know it won't be long before the temperature will drop, snow will fall and they won't be able to find their dinner. They stuff these nuts in the hollows of trees and other places so they can get to them later, when they will need them the most. The little munching thing they do with an acorn between their paws is their way of cleaning the morsel and leaving a scent so they can find their stash when winter comes.

There are several saving/investing lessons we can learn from these frisky little critters. The obvious ones are industry and thrift. Then there is diversification. These little guys don't just have one hiding place; biologists tell us they have hundreds! If they lose track of one spot, or if one cache is raided, no worries — they have several more. Ah! Diversification at work!

When you were in your accumulation years, were you busy like those little squirrels? I hope so. My father drummed into my head the importance of saving at least 10 percent of my earnings for, as he put it, a "rainy day." My first actual paycheck job was in Indiana when I was 18 years old, working for an ice cream shop. I felt as if I had joined the adult world. I made a whopping $150 per week. Seeing the paycheck stub was my first real foray into financial education. Part of my paycheck was missing! What was this thing called FICA that was eating part of my salary? When I asked what it meant, my supervisor said she didn't know, but that it was "withholding."

The concept of putting money aside for the future is, of course, is not easy for teens to grasp. After all, to them retirement seems as far away as a distant galaxy. The years whiz by very quickly, however. Before you know it, you are at that threshold where you say goodbye paycheck, hello retirement. The days of accumulation are over, and now it is time to do two things: (a) preserve what you have accumulated and (b) distribute it carefully so that it lasts the duration of your retirement.

Dollar-Cost Averaging

One of the beautiful things about being a young investor is that all you need to do is invest consistently over time. Because time is on your side, you benefit by this wonderful thing called "dollar-cost averaging."

If you have a job with an employer who offers a 401(k), you have an opportunity to contribute a certain amount of your paycheck to it every pay period. Please contribute the maximum if you possibly can. Moreover, if your employer has agreed to match your contribution, please take advantage of that. That's free money! You would be surprised at the number of young workers I meet who do not take advantage of this provision. In 2014, if you were under the age of 50, the maximum you could contribute to a 401(k) program was $17,500 per year. It is a win/win situation for you and your employer. The company gets a tax deduction for their share of the contribution, and you get to defer taxes on your portion. Money contributed to a 401(k) usually flows into an investment account which is managed by a custodian company. The custodian buys shares of mutual funds with the contribution.

Think of dollar-cost averaging this way: Your regular contribution goes into your 401(k) each time you receive a paycheck. The custodians of your account use that contribution to purchase as many shares of ABC mutual fund as that amount of money can buy. If ABC mutual fund shares increase in value, that's great! Your account value just went up. If the same shares decrease in value, that great too! Your contribution just bought more shares. Those skinny shares will fatten up some day. Remember, time is on your side. You are accumulating your retirement savings. The best thing you can do is keep saving. You are getting an overall average lower cost per share by doing nothing more than saving the same amount each period.

While this is true for younger investors, there comes a point in time when the winds shift and what once worked in your favor begins to work against you.

Reverse Dollar-Cost Averaging

When you stop working, you stop making those regular, steady contributions to your retirement fund, and, if you are like most folks, you begin taking regular, steady withdrawals instead. If you are writing yourself a paycheck to pay bills and meet expenses, which will usually be the same each month, then the money stream of your retirement account changes course and is now flowing backward. Instead of buying shares with your contributions, you are now selling shares with each withdrawal. If the withdrawals you need are the same amount each month, then you have no choice but to sell more shares when share prices go down. You can't time this fluctuation more now than you could when you were building your account. Every time the market goes down, you are hit by a double whammy — you have to sell more shares and when the market turns around there is much less in the account to take advantage of the upswing. In other words, market downturns hurt you much worse when you are taking withdrawals.

Know What Time It Is

Because I am a financial advisor, sometimes people will ask me, either in interviews or casual conversation, what general advice I would give to anyone wanting to be financially successful. I suppose it's a fair question, but the first time I heard it I was a little flummoxed. It's a little like asking a doctor what is the secret to good health. It's a very broad subject. Just as there are several factors that contribute to good physical health, there are myriad factors that contribute to good *fiscal* health. How do you put that in nugget form? But after giving it some thought I came up with a reply that as is true as it is concise: "Know what time it is, financially."

Some people don't seem to be aware of what time it is financially, and they invest the same way when they hit the retirement zone as they did when they were working. As we have said before, the methods and strategies that got you to retirement are likely not going to be the same ones you will need to get you through retirement. What a shame it would be to save for a number of years and then, due to some terrorist attack or a natural disaster halfway across the world, wake up to the news that the stock market has crashed and you have lost half your fortune. That is similar to what happened to many retirees and pre-retirees during the 2008 market crash. Young investors can recover from market corrections and even benefit from them. Older investors must be more cautious.

As the term "preservation phase" implies, we are at a point in our lives where we have accumulated some assets and don't wish to lose them. The famous American humorist Will Rogers (1879-1935) once remarked: "I'm more concerned about the return of my money than the return on my money." That echoes the sentiment of many who have worked their entire lives to accumulate a nest egg that they intend to carry them through their golden years. My council to you is, "don't take income from an account that goes up and down."

Bear Traps

The Standard & Poors (S&P) 500 is a stock market index based on the market capitalizations of 500 large companies having common stock listed on the New York Stock Exchange (NYSE) or Nasdaq. The research and analysis arm of the Standard & Poors defines a bear market as a period where the S&P 500 index drops more than 20 percent from the market's previous high. From 1950 – 2013 there were 10 bear markets.

A bear trap is when investors who are on the cusp of retirement have too much exposure in a volatile market and lose a significant portion of their portfolio in a bear market and have no time in which to recover their losses. I am sure that I, like many other financial advisors who specialize in retirement income planning, can point to case histories of individuals who came out of the 2008 stock market disaster financially battered and bruised. One case that sticks out in my mind was that of a woman who was making plans to retire at age 62. She was an event planner for a large corporation where she had been employed for 20 years. Year after year, she had contributed to her 401(k). No one cautioned her to begin making conservative choices in her allocations when she turned 60, and she saw no reason to do so.

"I was too busy working to pay attention to where the money in my retirement fund was invested," she said. "Then it was like all the clocks stopped at once and started moving backwards. I saw years of my hard-earned savings vanish overnight."

Looking back, the woman acknowledged that timing was the real culprit. Had the financial crisis and the recession which followed struck a year later she would have retired and rolled her 401(k) over to a secure, self-directed IRA. As it was, with over 40 percent of her nest egg gone, she had to stay at her job another five years to play catch up.

Recovery Time

There is much evidence to illustrate just how devastating the last bear market was to seniors who were exposed to too much risk. But the statistics make an even better case for seniors to exercise caution with investments when nearing retirement. The following data measures the Standard & Poor's 500 stock market index corrections from September 1929 to March 2009 (79 years):[30]

- There have been 16 bear markets since 1929.
- The average frequency of bear markets since 1929 is every 4.8 years.
- The average depth of a bear market since 1929 is 38.24 percent.
- The average duration of a bear market is 17 months.
- The average time to make up loss from a bear market is five years.
- In 47 out of 79 years (60 percent of the time), most investors have simply been making up losses. All new growth has occurred in just 40 percent of the time invested.

---

[30] Edward Yardeni, Joe Abbott and Mali Quintana. Yardeni Research, Inc. Nov. 17, 2016. http://www.yardeni.com/pub/sp500corrbear.pdf. Accessed Nov. 18, 2016.

S&P 500 Corrections
September 1929 through March 2009 (79 years)

Bear Market	Duration	Delcine	Time to Break Even
1. September 1929-June 1932	17 months	-86.00%	302 months
2. July 1933 – March 1935	20 months	-33.00%	28 months
3. March 1937 – March 1938	12 months	-54.00%	107 months
4. November 1938 – April 1942	41 months	-45.80%	77 months
5. May 1946 – March 1948	22 months	-28.10%	49 months
6. August 1956 – October 1957	14 months	-21.60%	25 months
7. December 1961 – June 1962	6 months	-28.00%	22 months
8. February 1966 – October 1966	8 months	-22.20%	16 months
9. November 1968 – May 1970	18 months	-36.10%	39 months
10. January 1973 – October 1974	21 months	-48.20%	25 months
11. November 1980 – August 1982	21 months	-27.10%	25 months
12. August 1987 – December 1987	3 months	-33.50%	23 months
13. July 1990 – October 1990	3 months	-19.90%	7 months
14. July 1998 – October 1998	3 months	-21.20%	3 months
15. March 2000 – October 2002	31 months	-49.10%	87 months
16. October 2007 – March 2009	17 months	-55.78%	Unknown

Source: www.standardandpoors.com

The "break even periods" shown here represent the amount of time it takes to gain back the ground lost during the bear market. Notice that some recessions are deeper than others are. For example, the 1987 bear market was brief (three months) but very deep (33.5 percent). Those who remember that correction may recall the numbers were back on the board pretty quickly, but because of the depth of the downturn, it took investors quite a while (almost two years) to get back to where they started.

Look at the bear market that lasted from March 2000 to October 2002. The S&P dropped 49.1 percent, and the down cycle lasted 31 months. It took investors more than seven years to rebound from that one. Once again, the key is timing. Bear markets are not kind to retirement nest eggs if the owner is at or near retirement. Do you have time to recover from a bear market that could last five years? Do you have the resources to weather such a storm? Those recovery times, by the way, are just getting back to the top of the cliff from which you descended — the "opportunity cost" of lost time and lost interest is another matter entirely. This is also without taking any money from your savings. Can you live without that for five years?

The Sequence of Returns Trap

Mark Twain said: "There are lies, damned lies and statistics."

One couple who sat down to review their dismal financial situation after the smoke cleared from the 2008 Wall Street debacle told me that when they asked their broker why he didn't prepare them for what could happen he said, "There's no need to worry about all that. Long term, the market will always produce a 10 percent return."

I'm not so sure about the 10 percent, but let's give the broker the benefit of the doubt on this one and round it off to 10 percent. Would you like to hear "the rest of the story," as the late Paul Harvey used to say? If you are 35 years old, that 10 percent average statistic may hold some water. But if your portfolio is a retirement portfolio and under the constant stress of systematic withdrawals, you must again consider the timing involved. In the investment world, it is known as the sequence of returns, and it makes all the difference in the world.

Sequence of returns is the order in which returns are realized. It matters big time if all your money is in the stock market and you are ready to retire, because losses impact your account more significantly. When you started out, time was on your side, and you could take the ups and downs of the market in stride. As previously mentioned during our discussion of dollar-cost averaging, you could even benefit from the volatility. But now that your cash river is flowing in the opposite direction, market losses just before or as you begin retirement can erase years of diligent savings.

Take the case of Bill and Bob for example. They each started out with the same amount ($500,000), they each retired at the same age (65), and they each had 100 percent of their assets in a brokerage account where it is subject to risk and volatility. To illustrate how much the sequence of returns can impact one's peace of mind and financial security in retirement, we are going to give them the same hypothetical market history, only at different times.

Both began withdrawing 5 percent each year from their accounts at age 65 and increasing their yearly withdrawals by 3 percent to accommodate inflation, and both averaged an 8.03 percent annual return. These returns are taken from an actual slice of historical returns. But the key here is that Bill and Bob had vastly different results because of when the market losses occurred. Bill took his losses in the beginning, when he was 65-67. In actual history, losses such as this occurred when the market crashed in 2000 with the bursting of the tech bubble. Bob experienced the same losses, only much later in retirement. Bill ran out of retirement savings at age 83 while Bob's still had plenty of money to fund his retirement.

Bill and Bob: A Hypothetical Market Timing Comparison

	BILL				BOB		
Age	Hypothetical stock market gains or losses	Withdrawal at start of year	Nest egg at start of year	Age	Hypothetical stock market gains or losses	Withdrawal at start of year	Nest egg at start of year
64			$500,000	64			$500,000
65	-10.14%	$25,000	$500,000	65	12.78%	$25,000	$500,000
66	-13.04%	$25,750	$426,839	66	23.45%	$25,750	$535,716
67	-23.37%	$26,523	$348,776	67	26.38%	$26,523	$629,575
68	14.62%	$27,318	$246,956	68	3.53%	$27,318	$762,140
69	2.03%	$28,138	$251,750	69	13.62%	$28,138	$760,755
70	12.40%	$28,982	$228,146	70	3.00%	$28,982	$832,396
71	27.25%	$29,851	$223,862	71	-38.49%	$29,851	$827,524
72	-6.65%	$30,747	$246,879	72	26.38%	$30,747	$490,684
73	26.31%	$31,669	$201,956	73	19.53%	$31,669	$581,270
74	4.46%	$32,619	$215,084	74	26.67%	$32,619	$656,916
75	7.06%	$33,598	$190,610	75	31.10%	$33,598	$790,788
76	-1.54%	$34,606	$168,090	76	20.26%	$34,606	$991,981
77	34.11%	$35,644	$131,429	77	34.11%	$35,644	$1,151,375
78	20.26%	$36,713	$128,458	78	-1.54%	$36,713	$1,496,314
79	31.01%	$37,815	$110,335	79	7.06%	$37,815	$1,437,133
80	26.67%	$38,949	$95,008	80	4.46%	$38,949	$1,498,042
81	19.53%	$40,118	$71,009	81	26.31%	$40,118	$1,524,231
82	26.38%	$36,923	$36,923	82	-6.56%	$41,321	$1,874,535
83	-38.49%	$0	$0	83	27.25%	$42,561	$1,712,970
84	3.00%			84	12.40%	$43,838	$2,125,604
85	13.62%			85	2.03%	$45,153	$2,339,923
86	3.53%			86	14.37%	$46,507	$2,341,297
87	26.38%			87	-23.27%	$47,903	$2,630,297
88	23.45%			88	-13.04%	$49,340	$1,978,993
89	12.78%			89	-10.14%	$50,820	$1,677,975
Average Return		Total Withdrawal		Average Return		Total Withdrawal	
8.03%		$580,963		8.03%		$911,482	

The Rule of 100

Wouldn't it be fantastic if we just had some kind of formula to keep us out of bear traps and sequence of returns trouble? In general, something that could tell us how much of our money we can safely keep at risk in retirement and how much we should keep completely safe? Well, there is — it's an investing rule of thumb called the "Rule of 100." Take your age and subtract it from 100. The result is the maximum percentage of your assets you should consider exposing to market risk. Another way to figure it is simply by putting a percent sign after your age.

Keep in mind it is called a rule of thumb. The expression goes back to the days before rulers and yardsticks when they would gauge things by the width or length of a body part. In the Bible, a cubit was the distance from your elbow to the tip of your middle finger. The width of a human thumb was used to approximate one inch. So this is not a hard and fast rule, only an approximation. Much of how closely you adhere to it has to do with your unique financial goals and circumstances. But let's say you are in your 70s, and you are thinking about your net worth and how much of your liquid assets are vulnerable to loss. How does it make you feel? If you are fine with it and can sleep well at night knowing that the news tomorrow could send the stock market into a tail spin, then you're fine! No adjustments necessary! But if you toss and turn and pace the floor worrying about such an eventuality, then some adjustments are in order.

By the same token, if you are age 25 and you don't have 75 percent of your money aggressively working for you, then you, too, probably need to make some adjustments. I call it having "fiscal symmetry."

CHAPTER FIVE

What You Need to Know About Social Security

"Should any political party attempt to abolish social security, unemployment insurance, and eliminate labor laws and farm programs, you would not hear of that party again in our political history."

~ Dwight D. Eisenhower

To what extent can a retiree rely on Social Security? If you are a baby boomer, you may remember your parents signing up to receive their Social Security benefits when they turned 65. Or maybe they elected to take it early at age 62. Either way, there was little doubt about the soundness of the program. Today, some wonder if Social Security will be there for them and at what age they should take it. Have you looked at a Social Security statement lately? There is an ominous message that appears on the front page of the statement under the heading "What Social Security Means to You." The SSA's message should make boomers sigh with relief for themselves and perhaps develop a little frown of worry for their adult children.

About Social Security's future...

Social Security is a compact between generations. Since 1935, America has kept the promise of security for its workers and their families. Now, however, the Social Security system is facing serious financial problems, and action is needed soon to make sure the system will be sound when today's younger workers are ready for retirement.

Without changes, in 2033 the Social Security Trust Fund will be able to pay only about 77 cents for each dollar of scheduled benefits.* We need to resolve these issues soon to make sure Social Security continues to provide a foundation of protection for future generations."

*Source: http://www.socialsecurity.gov/policy/docs/ssb/v70n3/v70n3p111.html

---

So the doom and gloom predictions about Social Security are not without foundation. It's just not an immediate problem. With no changes, the system will function as is until 2033. So that pretty much lets baby boomers off the hook, doesn't it? It's the children of boomers who will see a different Social Security landscape. Higher taxes, lower benefits, higher age for qualification? Maybe a combination of all of those things?

When Can I Sign Up? When Should I?

An excellent question, and one on the minds of many who turn 62, is, "When should I begin collecting my Social Security benefits?" For many years, full retirement age (called "normal retirement age" by the Social Security Administration, or "NRA") was 65. But beginning with people born in 1938 or later, that age gradually increases until it reaches 67. That's how it stands at this writing, anyway — it could change in the future.

But there's more to it than that. For example, if your spouse dies, you qualify to receive Social Security at age 60. The longer you wait to collect, however, the larger your benefit will be, until you reach age 70.

There are all sorts of caveats, rules and exceptions to the rules, so if you fall into any of the categories we will briefly touch on here, I suggest you go to www.ssa.gov and read up on it. You may find it useful to pull your own Social Security statement and examine it.

Just because your NRA is 66, for example, does not mean that you have to wait until you are 66 to

Age To Receive Full Social Security Benefits (Called "full retirement age" or normal retirement age.)	
Year of Birth*	**Full Retirement Age**
1937 or earlier	65
1938	65 and 2 months
1939	65 and 4 months
1940	65 and 6 months
1941	65 and 8 months
1942	65 and 10 months
1943-1954	66
1955	66 and 2 months
1956	66 and 4 months
1957	66 and 6 months
1958	66 and 8 months
1959	66 and 10 months
1960 and later	67

*If you were born on January 1st of any year you should refer to the previous year. (If you were born on the 1st of the month, we figure your benefit (and your full retirement age) as if your birthday was in the previous month.)

Source: Social Security Administration

begin collecting your benefits. You can do that as early as age 62. But should you? Well, it depends. Do you desperately need the money? Are you seriously ill? Then maybe you should. From a planning perspective, that is, when you are trying to squeeze the most guaranteed income out of the system as possible, you may find it useful to wait as long as possible before claiming benefits. Why? Because the earlier you claim below the age of 70, the more reduced your benefits will be. Think of it this way. Every year you wait between your full retirement age and 70 to take your benefits, they increase by approximately 8 percent per year.

As to the dollar amount, this will be different for each individual. It's all based on how much you paid into the system and how long you worked. The best way to get those numbers is to go to www.ssa.gov and get your benefit amount. One of the first boxes to greet you is "My Social Security." This is where you can answer a few questions and establish your own account. The statement will give you the dollar amount if you start collecting as soon as you are eligible, when you are at full retirement age, when you turn 70, and at any interval in between.

As far as I can tell, baby boomers appear to be in good shape when it comes to receiving their Social Security benefits. What's in store for those in their 30s and 40s is hard to say. Social Security will most likely still be here, but probably not in its present form. We do know there will be fewer workers supporting a much larger retired population and that, more than ever, the financial burden of retirement clearly lies with you. If you don't have a written plan on how to optimize your Social Security benefit, please contact your financial professional.

Taxes on Social Security

The story goes that as Franklin Delano Roosevelt was signing his name to the document that would launch the Social Security Act of 1935, reporters asked him if he would ever tax Social Security benefits. The word is he pounded the desk in the oval office and bellowed, "I will never tax Social Security!" Whether FDR actually said those words or not (the Social Security Administration says not), he never did tax Social Security benefits. President Roosevelt died of a cerebral hemorrhage on April 12, 1945, at his cottage in Warm Springs, Georgia. Legislation that would call for taxing a portion of Social Security benefits would be enacted almost 50 years and eight presidents later under the administration of the "Great Communicator," Ronald Reagan, who signed into law the Social Security Amendments of 1983. That law stated that if your base annual income was $25,000 as a single taxpayer, or $32,000 as a married couple filing jointly, then up to 50 percent of your Social Security income would be treated as taxable income. Ten years later, when President Bill Clinton was in office, the law was revised, raising taxation to up to 85 percent of benefits for single beneficiaries with incomes over $34,000, and couples earning more than $44,000. As of this writing, that's where it stands.[31]

---

[31] Social Security Administration. "Social Security History." https://www.social security.gov/history/. Accessed Nov. 18, 2016.

Taxable Social Security[32]

-	Income	Percentage of Social Security Taxable
Single, Head of Houshold, Qualifying Widower and Married Filing Seperately (where the spouses lived apart the entire year)	Below $25,000	All SS income is tax-free
	$25,000 - $34,000	Up to 50% of SS income may be taxable
	$34,000 and up	Up to 85% of SS income may be taxable
Married Filing Jointly	Below $32,000	All SS income is tax-free
	$32,000 - $44,000	Up to 50% of SS income may be taxable
	$44,000 and up	Up to 85% of SS income may be taxable

* Note:

Your adjusted gross income

+ Nontaxable interest

+ ½ of your Social Security benefits

= Your "**combined income**"

Before I continue on this theme, let me make one thing perfectly clear (my apologies to Mr. Nixon). I love the red white and blue, and I am as patriotic as the next person. I don't mind paying my fair share of taxes; I just don't want to pay more than my fair share, and I don't think you should have to either. Because we deal with such matters, an old joke accountants tell from time to time goes: "What's the difference between tax evasion and tax avoidance? About 15 years."

Tax avoidance is the use of legal means to reduce the amount of tax you owe. All citizens have the right to do this, and there is nothing unethical, illegal or shady about it. Tax evasion, on the other hand, is an illegal practice

---

[32] Mark P. Cussen. Investopedia. Jan. 7, 2008. "Avoid the Social Security Tax Trap." http://www.investopedia.com/articles/pf/08/social-security-tax.asp. Accessed Nov. 18, 2016.

where people fraudulently avoid paying their true tax liability. If you just got a mental picture of Al Capone in handcuffs, we are on the same page.

So how do you avoid paying taxes on your Social Security income? Well, you may not be able to. It all depends on what goes onto the taxable income line on your 1040 form each year. Some people drop their jaw when they learn that the IRS does not necessarily consider all income reportable income. They spell all this out, by the way, in the IRS tax code — you just have to know where to look. Parenthetically, if the IRS tax code were a book, it would be twice as thick as Leo Tolstoy's "War and Peace," the universal iconic standard for thick books. Within the IRS code, hiding in plain sight, are golden, tax-saving nuggets that can save ordinary taxpayers thousands of dollars.

Some examples of reportable income for the purpose of calculating taxes on Social Security benefits include such things as:
- Interest from bank CDs
- Income from investments, such as stocks and mutual funds
- Income from tax-free municipal bonds (yes, it's true)
- Income from pensions
- Withdrawals from IRAs or other tax-deferred plans
- Salaries and tips
- State tax refunds (if you itemized last year)

You would be amazed at how many people report just a few hundred dollars over the limits described above and, in so doing, trigger taxes on their Social Security. A strategy the IRS provides (but is not putting up billboards about), is simply moving assets from taxable to tax-deferred investments. Imagine two buckets. One bucket says "taxable" and the other bucket says "tax-deferred." It is really about as simple as that. Not everyone can do it, and each case is different. But you may be able to switch buckets (the vehicles holding your investments) and avoid paying unnecessary taxes. Unless you are actually receiving the income, the IRS may not even count this as reportable income. Fixed and fixed indexed annuities are popular tax-deferred buckets because you never pay taxes on your annuity gains until you start taking distributions. This is not the case with interest earned by CDs or from brokerage accounts — such gains are fully reportable and taxable in the year in which they occur. Make no mistake, you will eventually pay taxes on fixed and indexed annuity gains. Tax-deferred means taxes are postponed. But the more income you can move to the unreportable side of the tax return form, the further away you stand from Social Security taxation.

In case you are wondering why every overpaying Social Security recipient is not at least looking into the possibility of "switching buckets," it is because most of them just aren't aware these strategies exist. According to the Federal Reserve Survey of Consumer Services, only 25 percent of Americans have a financial advisor and not all financial advisors know the tax code inside and out, although, in my opinion, they should. I advise anyone considering making such changes to consult with a tax professional first. This is because every case is different, and the tax professional can inform you accurately as to whether such a move is in compliance and is in your best interest.[33]

---

[33] Jeff Larrimore, Mario ArthurBentil, Sam Dodini, and Logan Thomas. Board of Governors of the Federal Reserve System. May 2015. "Report on the Economic Well-Being of U.S. Households in 2014."

Phantom Income

The term "phantom income" sounds a bit scary, doesn't it? Phantom income is defined as income that is reported to the IRS as if you received it, even if you never saw it and didn't spend it. If you own equities, for example, and you sell off shares of those holdings at a profit without actually pulling those profits from the account, do you still owe taxes on those gains? Yes.

"You mean even if I left the money in the account?"

Yes. Uncle Sam does not care. You still owe taxes on those gains.

With mutual funds, for example, you have a manager who may make several stock trades a year, ostensibly with the aim of selecting stocks that will produce growth. When fund managers sell stocks within the portfolio at a profit, that registers as a gain and is credited to you as income, even if it never entered your checking account and you did not withdraw the profit. IRS rules say you pay taxes on it anyway, even if you left it in the account.

One way to eliminate that tax obligation is to move the money into a tax-deferred vehicle, such as an indexed annuity. It is perfectly legal and ethical to use these provisions. They are clearly written in legible type. Unfortunately, you will not see a section in the IRS code entitled "Tax Breaks." And they aren't "loopholes," either. They are IRS "provisions." You just have to know where to find them.

CHAPTER SIX

The Four Percent Rule and Other Investment Myths

"There are no sure bets in the world of investing; there is risk in everything. Be prepared for the ups and downs."

~ Jim Kramer

The greatest fear seniors have these days is outliving their resources. According to one survey, the fear of running out of money in old age ranked ahead of all other phobias, even the fear of dying. The fear is not so much about cash as it is losing one's independence and becoming a burden to loved ones.[34]

In 1994, a California financial planner named William P. Bengen came up with an investing formula that he said would solve the problem. It came to be known as the "Prudent Man's Rule" or "the Four Percent Sustainable Withdrawal Rule," and finally just the "Four Percent Rule." The idea behind the magic formula was that if retirees kept all their assets in a carefully managed brokerage account and withdrew 4 percent of it each year during their retirement, their money should last them for at least 30 years. The formula called for rebalancing the nest egg periodically and adjusting the withdrawal amount each year for inflation. The only problem was, it didn't hold up when put into practice. The 4 percent withdrawal concept, once regarded as the Holy Grail of retirement investing by stockbrokers and other Wall Street types, has come to be viewed as a flawed formula and many, but not all, believers have left the church. Nobel Prize winning economist William Sharpe had this to say about it:

"Supporting a constant spending plan using a volatile investment policy is fundamentally flawed. A retiree using a 4 percent rule faces spending shortfalls when risky investments underperform, may accumulate wasted surpluses when they outperform and, in any case, could likely

---

[34] Allianz Life Insurance Company of North America. June 17, 2010. "Reclaiming the Future." http://www.retirementmadesimpler.org/Library/ENT-991.pdf. Accessed Dec. 5, 2016.

purchase exactly the same spending distributions more cheaply."[35]

Bengen, who is now retired, based his findings on research performed at a time when the stock market knew only one direction — up. He took a portfolio of 50 percent stocks and 50 percent bonds and ran it through a slew of market scenarios. He analyzed returns going back to 1926 in 30-year spans, all in an attempt to find the correct rate of withdrawal that would not deplete the nest egg. The theory was that the growth of the account would offset the withdrawals enough so that, with continual rebalancing, the account would provide a virtually never-ending wellspring of funds if kept to a constant flow. In fairness to Bengen and the other bright minds who worked on the formula, it would have worked if the stock market had continued to behave in the 2000s the way it had behaved in the 1990s. In those heady days, virtually any stock you picked was an instant winner, and investors were chasing down stocks ending in dot-com as if they were a sure bet. In those days, quarterly 401(k) statements were a pleasure to open and see how much fatter your retirement account had become. As a result, stockbrokers were on the same level of popularity as astronauts.

Then came the jolt of the dot-com crash in 2000, exposing the soft underbelly of the stock market. The 1980s and 1990s had seen one of the longest economic expansions in United States history, but that was over. Many on Wall Street simply could not accept the fact that the party had ended, and the rules had changed. They insisted on holding onto the Four Percent Withdrawal Rule in spite of the mounting evidence that it no longer worked. The mantra of

---

[35] Jason S. Scott, William F. Sharpe and John G. Watson. Standford.edu. April 2008. "The 4% Rule – At What Price?" https://web.stanford.edu/~wfsharpe/retecon/4percent .pdf.

these priests of Wall Street seemed to be: "The stock market giveth, and the stock market taketh away. Blessed be the name of the stock market." They are right in a sense because the behavior of the stock market from 2000 to 2010 was like that of a toddler who can't decide if he wants to play inside or outside — up one day and down the next with wild swings in either direction. Plenty of activity but, from a profit point of view, little accomplishment. When the dust settled, and the smoke cleared at the end of that 10-year period, the market ended virtually where it had started. Even die-hard adherents to the 4 percent rule had to admit that the math no longer worked.

As we saw in the previous chapter, timing is everything if you intend to retire on a nest egg that is invested solely in bonds and mutual funds. If you were to lose 40 percent of your retirement investment savings within a year or two of your retirement, the 4 percent rule would make you penniless rather quickly. Let's say, for example, that you had retired on Jan. 1, 2000, for example, with a portfolio of 55 percent stocks and 45 percent bonds and then rebalanced the portfolio each month, increasing the withdrawal amount by 3 percent each year for inflation, as the 4 percent rule advocates. Your portfolio would still have fallen by a third at the end of 2010. Investment firm T. Rowe Price estimated that your chances of making it through three decades of retirement would only be 29 percent. When you put it that way, it makes it pretty obvious that the 4 percent rule is not the retirement vehicle to get you where you want to go, doesn't it? It would be like boarding a plane only to hear the pilot say, "Welcome aboard. We have a 29 percent chance of arriving at our destination." How long would it take you to decide not to fly that airline?[36]

What Is the Solution?

The solution is to look for approaches that work and get rid of the ones that don't. We do that with other aspects of our lives. Kelley Greene, a reporter for the Wall Street Journal, wrote an article that appeared in the March 1, 2013, edition of the WSJ, suggesting the use of annuities with income riders. She quotes Wade Pfau, a professor who researches retirement income at the American College of Financial Services in Bryn Mawr, Pennsylvania. Professor Pfau plotted how 1,001 different product allocations might work for a 65-year-old married couple hoping to generate 4 percent annual income from their portfolio. Using 200 Monte Carlo simulations for each product, and assuming returns based on current market conditions, the winning combination turned out to be a 50/50 mix of stocks and fixed annuities. "Annuities, with their promise of income for life, act like "super bonds with no maturity dates," says Pfau, who holds a Ph.D. in economics from Princeton University.[37]

My personal observation is that, in the face of the facts, more and more financial advisors are recommending annuities. One reason is the demand by modern retirees for guarantees. The Four Percent Rule was based on projec-

---

[36] T. Rowe Price Associates. January 2011. "Dismal Decade Offers Cautionary Lessons for Retirees." https://www4.troweprice.com/iws/wps/wcm/connect/e3c2ec80459 61707ba69bf32e4e97423/DismalDecade.pdf?MOD=AJPERES. Accessed Nov. 18, 2016.

[37] Kelley Greene. The Wall Street Journal. March 1, 2013. "Say Goodbye to the 4% Rule." http://www.wsj.com/articles/SB100014241278873241623045783044914925 59684. Accessed Nov. 18, 2016.

tions. If the market crashes of the 2000 decade proved anything, it was that projections can fail. Not even the brightest financial minds can foretell the future. Even though the stock market has made spectacular gains since the depths of the economic crisis that shook Wall Street in 2009, the aftershocks still linger in the minds of many of baby boomers. Like earthquake survivors, they remain fearful, with good reason, that it could happen again and without warning. Those who saw their nest eggs implode look at annuities and the income guarantees that come with them as quite desirable by contrast. Now that they are retiring, it's not so much the return on their investment that they worry about as it is the return of their investment. Since gambling on the stock market has fallen out of favor with boomers, and they are looking for guarantees, it is no wonder that the term "indexed annuity" is surfacing more and more in conversations with once market-bound financial advisors. Ifs and maybes are great for talking purposes, but for the nuts and bolts of retirement planning, you need guarantees

The "Buy and Hold" Theory

There may have been a time in America when you could buy into a few mutual funds and sit back and watch them grow. This method of investing is called "buy and hold." This may have worked back when the stock market would recede and advance in predictable patterns like ocean tides, but the 21st century stock market is much too volatile to trust with a buy and hold approach. Times have changed. A disturbance in one hemisphere is instantly registered on another hemisphere, oceans away. Markets react with lightning speed, and trading is done instantly on computers. Establishing a position in the market and checking on it a year later is putting your portfolio in danger.

The idea behind the "buy and hold" strategy is simply to keep the faith and hold the line when the giants of Wall Street are begging for bailouts and the market is crashing. That is the theme music for stockbrokers when their clients are hurting. When clients are asking why they are losing years' worth of diligent savings in a matter of weeks, they usually hear the same old one-liners every time:

"Don't feel like the Lone Ranger."

"All boats go down when the tide goes out."

"Don't worry, everyone lost money in this one."

Another one-liner brokers use is, "Just hang in there; the market will bounce back." That one is usually true. For every market loss there is a market recovery. But as previously pointed out in this book, timing is everything when investing is involved. Those who are on the cusp of retiring may not have time to benefit from a market recovery. For them, using a buy-and-hold strategy in a volatile market could be like playing with a loaded revolver. Those that do recover have also lost all that time.

Twenty-first-century asset protection calls for more than just strategic asset allocation. Commissioned stockbrokers like to point to a menu and say, "See, we have you in large cap funds, small cap funds, international funds, bond funds and growth stocks. You are diversified." Correction. You are not diversified. All that means is that your eggs are in different locations in the same basket. The modern way to protect your assets from negative returns early in your retirement (the iceberg to your retirement Titanic) is through product allocation, which is a placing your assets in a number of dissimilar investment vehicles. Some of them may be market-based, and others may be guaranteed, fixed-rate investments. It all depends on your unique, individual financial situation.

When I was 5 years old, to keep me busy, my grandfather would give me a small hammer and a board with about 20 small nails started in it. My "job" as his helper was to pound the nails the rest of the way into the board. The task would keep me busy and out of his hair for about 30 minutes. What would have happened had my grandfather handed me a screwdriver instead of a hammer? I may have gotten a few nails in, or I might have hurt myself. The point is, the correct tool for the job was a hammer, not a screwdriver. Your retirement accounts are the same way. Use mutual funds for accumulation; that is the purpose for which they are designed. Only accounts with guarantees should be used for income. My recommendation is, "Do not take income from accounts that go up and down."

CHAPTER SEVEN

What Is Your Number for Retirement?

"The question isn't at what age I want to retire, it's at what income."

~George Foreman

One question I hear quite often is "How much do I need to have saved up before I can retire?" The conversation may go something like this:

Client: "I've got $400,000 in my 401(k) plan. That's enough to retire on isn't it?"

Me: "Do you know how much you will need to withdraw from that account each month to cover your living expenses?

Client: "I don't know. I guess I'll just take out what I need when I need it. That's almost a half million ... shouldn't that last a long time?"

Me: "How long do you think your retirement will last?"

Client: "I plan on living a long time!"

Me: "If you spend $40,000 per year your money will be gone in 10 years."

Client: "But won't my money keep on growing while I am spending it?"

And here is where I give the answer that I should have given in the first place, because it is the only true answer anyone can give to a question like this — "It depends."

Without all the facts, it is impossible to answer questions of strategy — accurately, anyway — any other way.

Imagine someone turning on a faucet to fill up a bathtub and asking, "Will this be enough to fill the tub?" The answer is, "It depends. It depends on how long you run the water. It depends on your interpretation of "full." It depends on whether the drain is open or closed.

When it comes to planning for retirement, there is no easy fix, no magic formula, no silver bullet, no one-size-fits-all. It all depends. One thing is certain, however: guessing isn't planning. For that matter, neither is hoping. Proper planning for retirement is defined by two words that have a non-fun, almost medicinal sound — analysis and calculation.

"How About a Gazillion?"

Whoever invented the digital video recorder should have won the Nobel Peace prize. My TV watching time is minimal to begin with but sitting through five minutes of commercials to watch five minutes of evening news is nerve-jangling. Therefore, I usually record such programs and fly through the ads.

One commercial that caught my attention recently, however, was one about finding "your number" for retirement. It was clever and made a very good point, I thought. The 30-second spot started out with a man walking his dog down a tree-lined street with an oversized orange number under his arm. The thing must have been made out of Styrofoam. I couldn't make out the number, but it was seven digits... a little over a million. He waves hello to a man who is obviously a neighbor. The neighbor is on a ladder trimming a hedge. On the top of the hedge sits the word "Gazillion," also in big Styrofoam letters, painted yellow and trimmed in purple. The incongruity of these two fellows and these large numbers is, of course, what catches your eye and makes you wonder what's going on.

Hedge trimmer: "Hey Clark. Whatcha got there?"

Dog walker: "It's my number. It's the amount I need to save to retire the way I want to. Is that your number, Gazillion?"

Hedge trimmer: "Yeah, gazillion, bazillion... It's just a guess."

Dog walker: "How do you plan for that?

Hedge trimmer: (nervous laugh) "I just blindly throw money at it and hope something good happens."

Dog walker: "So you really don't have a plan at all."

Hedge trimmer: (embarrassed look, nervous laugh) "I really don't."

I can't remember who produced the commercial — probably a big insurance company — but it makes a great point. To have an effective plan for retiring you first must come up with your own individual number — the amount you will need to pay bills and maintain your desired standard of living for the rest of your life. If you don't, you are just like the hedge-trimming neighbor — aimlessly hoping you will get by. And once you have it, how do you turn it into income forever?

Know Where You Are

Have you ever seen those little information booths in the middle of large shopping malls that tell you how the stores are laid out and where everything is? They usually have a red arrow or a red dot that says "You Are Here." The inference is the first order of business in getting where you want to go is to know where you are. Getting to "your number" in retirement starts with an analysis of what your assets are and where you have placed them.

The next logical step is determining how you wish to live in retirement. Aside from being able to eat, sleep in a comfortable bed and pay your bills, what do you wish to do? Travel? Play with the grandchildren? Take up golf? Once you have the total income you will need, the next step is to calculate how much you will need to get you where you want to go.

I realize this is easier said than done, but this is how you come up with your own, unique "number." As you can see, you don't pluck it out of thin air, or guess at it like our hedge trimming friend. You back into it mathematically.

Other Sources of Income

Your unique number will also include other calculations, such as how much income you expect to receive from other sources during your retirement. What about Social Security? I encourage people to go to the Social Security Administration website, www.socialsecurity.gov/myaccount, and set up their personal account. Knowing this number will help you make other decisions. The site is secure and relatively easy to navigate. The hardest part is plugging in all the information. You will need your Social Security number, date of birth, mailing address and email address, of course. Then there are the security questions so no one can access your account but you. Make sure you write down your password and put it somewhere retrievable; if you enter the wrong one three times it will lock you out for three days.

The first thing you will notice is how well Uncle Sam has kept track of you throughout your life. Every job and how much income you reported since you started — it's all there. You can also see how much your estimated Social Security benefits will be if you begin receiving them at various ages. This is an important piece of information if you are trying to come up with your "number." You will also see a very clear explanation of exactly how your Social Security benefits are calculated.

You may also have income from investments or rental properties. Charting this may require some professional help if you are not exactly sure of how much your investments will generate in the way of interest and dividends, or if you are uncomfortable with projections and would prefer guarantees.

Different Strokes for Different Folks

So how much money do you need to retire, live comfortably and sleep well at night? I realize people would much prefer a neat and tidy number or formula instead of hearing "it depends," but... It depends! A lot of it depends on your personal timeline. The earlier you plan to retire the more money you will need. I know plenty of people who, after doing the analysis and the calculations, had a choice to make. Would they (a) pare down their lifestyle to make it match their assets? Or would they (b) continue working until their assets could match their desired lifestyle? As they say, different strokes for different folks.

To estimate the retirement savings needed to retire, a rough rule of thumb goes something like this. Take the amount of annual income you will need in retirement and multiply it by 20 if you are retiring in your mid-to-late 60s. Multiply by 25 if you're retiring in your late 50s or early 60s. Remember, this is a general rule of thumb.

Could I make a suggestion at this point? You don't go it alone when it comes to your health. I don't think you will find a website or a book entitled, "Do-It-Yourself Dentistry." I doubt that Barnes & Nobel will feature "Self-Surgery for Dummies" on their book-of-the-month list. You consult with medical professionals when your health is concerned. It should be the same way with your wealth — especially where retirement is concerned. Consult with a professional before making these crucial decisions regarding your financial future. The first thing a competent doctor will do is interview you and ascertain your condition. A doctor will spend much more time listening and analyzing before offering you a course of treatment or a prescription, and that's how it should be.

Likewise, a financial professional will spend more time listening and asking questions before making any recommendations. That is why the first visit to a retirement income planner is called a "consultation," and is likely to be free of charge. It is a good time to determine if the professional can help or not. Sometimes there is no point in going past the consulting appointment. In most instances, however, the appointment will prove worth the time.

No one I am acquainted with has ever planned to fail at anything. Not intentionally anyway. But there is an adage, "failing to plan is planning to fail." In other words, the failure happens by default. Surveys reveal that about half of all American workers who qualify to be called "senior citizens" have taken steps to prepare a financial analysis to be like "Clark," the dog-walker in the commercial I mentioned earlier, and determine what size their retirement nest egg needs to be.[38]

I like the way Steve Vernon, research scholar for the Stanford Center on Longevity put it: "I'm reminded of the adage 'nobody plans to fail, but many fail to plan.' Having a good plan gives you the confidence to enjoy a healthy, meaningful rest-of-life. Surveys show that only about half of older workers prepare a financial analysis to determine the size of their retirement nest egg. Are you in the smart half, and if yes, how do you prepare your analyses?"[39]

---

[38] CFP Board. Sept. 24, 2015. "Survey: Americans' Use of Financial Advisors, CFP® Professionals Rises; Agree Advice Should Be in Their Best Interest." http://www.cfp.net/news-events/latest-news/2015/09/24/survey-americans-use-of-financial-advisors-cfp-professionals-rises-agree-advice-should-be-in-their-best-interest. Accessed Nov. 18, 2016.

[39] Steve Vernon. Moneywatch and CBS News. Feb. 3, 2010. "How Much Retirement Savings Do You Need?" http://www.cbsnews.com/news/how-much-retirement-savings-do-you-need/. Accessed Nov. 18, 2016.

CHAPTER EIGHT

What People Think About Annui- ties and Why

"The world is full of magic things, patiently waiting for our senses to grow sharper."

~W. B. Yeats

O ne interesting take on Americans' love/hate relation- ship with annuities is the article, "An Annuity by Any Other Name." The title was a takeoff on a line from William Shakespeare's famous "Romeo and Juliet." Juliet, a Capulet, and Romeo, a Montague, are lovers despite their feuding families (think Hatfields and McCoys). In Act II, Scene II, Juliet implores Romeo to look only at the love they share. The entire line is:

'Tis but thy name that is my enemy;
Thou art thyself, though, not a Montague.
What's Montague? It is nor hand, nor foot,
Nor arm, nor face, nor any other part
Belonging to a man. O, be some other name!
What's in a name? That which we call a rose
By any other name would smell as sweet.

As puzzling as it may be, some people swear at annuities and some people swear by them. There seems to be no middle ground. In "An Annuity by Any Other Name," the writer describes how Allianz Life Insurance Company of North America, one of the leading providers of fixed annuities in the world, did a survey and found 54 percent of those surveyed expressed a negative opinion about annuities, "even after describing an annuity-like solution as their ideal financial vehicle." Makes you wonder where the disconnect is, doesn't it?[40]

Once when I was speaking to a small group of investors, I tried a little experiment. I described all the features of a fixed indexed annuity, one by one, without telling the group the name of the financial vehicle. After each feature, I asked for a thumbs up or thumbs down vote. Here were their responses:

- Lifetime income – thumbs up.
- Safety of principal – thumbs up.
- Gains track upward movement of a market index – thumbs up.
- No losses when market goes down – thumbs up.

---

[40] Joe Mont. The Street. Sept. 9, 2010. "An Annuity by Any Other Name." http://www.thestreet.com/story/10855285/1/an-annuity-by-any-other-name-.html. Accessed Nov. 18, 2016.

- Gains lock in every year – thumbs up.
- Balance of account goes to heirs when you die – thumbs up.

The more I talked about the fixed indexed annuity without using the phrase "fixed indexed annuity," the more enthusiasm the small group seemed to have for it, whatever "it" was. Then I told them that no product is perfect, and they nodded in agreement. I explained that this product had a trade-off. In return for solid growth potential with no possibility of loss due to market volatility, there was a penalty for early withdrawal. They all said that was understandable. Thumbs up again!

"How important is liquidity to you?" I asked the group.

They all felt that liquidity was important to them. I asked if they would be satisfied with 10 percent free withdrawals every contract year for the first 10 years and then unlimited after that in return for no downside risk. They all said that seemed like a fair trade-off.

Then I asked straightforwardly, "How many here like fixed indexed annuities?"

Most thumbs went down. Only a few thumbs pointed upward. I would later learn that the upturned thumbs belonged to people who owned annuities and were satisfied with their performance.

So what does that tell us? That in our hurry to label and pigeonhole things, we can "throw the baby out with the bathwater" if we are not careful.

The Sentiment Behind the Word

Remember flash cards from elementary school? When the teacher flashes a word, a mental picture pops into your head — and usually a sentiment along with it.

SNAKE – Yuk!

BUTTERFLY – Ahh!

It's involuntary and entirely emotionally driven. We form our opinions, correct or incorrect, often with prejudicial conclusions based on what we think to be true. Can that also apply to financial terms? Absolutely!

Take the word, "bank" for example. Most people have a positive response to the word "bank." Perhaps because it signifies a secure place to put money. A place we trust. "You can take that to the bank." "You can bank on that."

Our impressions may go all the way back to our childhood. Remember piggy banks growing up? I loved mine. It was a pink, ceramic, hollow pig about the size of a football. When aunts and uncles came to visit, they would sometimes put a few quarters, or even a folded up bill or two, into "Miss Piggy."

Later on in life, I started a checking account and a savings account and deposited my paychecks into a real bank. I gave very little thought to what they did with the money. All I knew was when I made a withdrawal, the money was there. I trusted the bank.

Banks seem to go out of their way to select names that engender trust. Names like "First National Bank and Trust," or "First Federal Savings and Loan." To my knowledge, no banks are named, "Bob and Ethel's Take-a-Chance Bank." Have you noticed that banks like the word, "first" in their name? Americans like things that are first. One bank name has always puzzled me — "Fifth Third Bank" (I'm serious). The point I am making is names are important when it comes to things financial. Sometimes we will base our actions involving thousands of dollars on little more than the sound of a name.

While the word "bank" may conjure up pleasant memories for us, not so for people who lived through the 1930s and the Great Depression, when bank failures were a common occurrence. According to the Federal Deposit Insurance Corporation (FDIC) — the institution that has in-sured banks since 1933, as many as 4,000 banks went belly-up from 1929-1933, costing depositors an estimated $1.3 billion. After the Banking Act of 1933 established the FDIC, trust slowly returned. Some, however, vowed never to trust again, preferring to bury their money under a rock in the back yard rather than ever do business with a bank again.[41]

The Word, "Annuity"

One reason some people want to pick up the nearest sharp object when you say the word "annuity" may involve a negative experience they have had with variable annui-ties. Suze Orman and I don't see eye-to-eye on every-thing, but I have to agree with her on variable annuities. When an interviewer from CNNMoney.com asked the TV personality what she thought of them, she minced no words.

"I hate variable annuities," Orman said, gesturing em-phatically. "Especially variable annuities that are used in retirement accounts."

Orman went on to blast variable annuities for the high fees associated with the mutual funds in which they invest and for the mortality expenses associated with the insur-ance features — Charges that she says eat away at your gains. Orman also decried what she feels like is a "little white lie" brokers tell clients when selling them a variable annuity. "They tell you that you can never get back less than what you put into the [variable] annuity," Orman says.

---

[41] Bill Ganzel. Ganzel Group and Wessels Living History Farm. 2003. "Farming in the 1930s: Bank Failures." http://www.livinghistoryfarm.org/farminginthe30s/money _08.html. Accessed Nov. 18, 2016.

"What they don't tell you is that you have to die for that to happen."

Variable Annuities Can Lose Money

Variable annuities are stock market investment vehicles in an insurance wrapper. Why? Why not just put your money directly in the stock market? Because annuities have the advantage of tax-deferral. With an ordinary brokerage account, you must pay income taxes on your gains as you go. Those funds cannot be working for you if they are in the federal tax coffers. With a variable annuity, however, the gains are plowed back into the contract and, if the market goes up, can continue working for you. The downside is that when the market goes down, the variable annuity loses. A special provision can be attached to the variable annuity (for a fee) that acts like a life insurance policy. It guarantees that, regardless of how much your variable annuity loses, your beneficiary will receive at least as much as you deposited into the contract. As Suze Orman points out, that's fine for the ones you leave behind but it doesn't do you much good when you're living.

Keep in mind, the variable annuity is the only type of annuity where the principal, or original amount deposited, is at risk.

Types of Annuities

All poodles are dogs but not all dogs are poodles.

All Fords are cars, but not all cars are Fords.

There are many different varieties of annuities. It is easy, without digging a little deeper, to confuse one type of annuity with another, or to judge all annuities by the characteristics of one or two.

Traditional Fixed Annuity

We use the word "traditional" here to set this annuity type apart from all modified versions that come from it. The traditional fixed annuity follows the original basic concept used by the Romans around the time of Christ. The owner of the fixed annuity (annuitant) receives a yearly payout, guaranteed for a specified period (usually for life) in return for a lump sum. These annuities provide a guaranteed interest rate. Typically, that rate is adjusted each year. Most contracts have a minimum guaranteed rate — called a floor — that the rate cannot fall below. Most start the fixed annuity with a lump sum with the option of adding to it over time.

Traditional fixed annuities resemble a bank certificate of deposit only with a higher rate of return. You give your chunk of money (premium) to an insurance company instead of a bank. The insurance company promises you a declared interest rate for a term, which is typically much higher than what a bank offers on CDs. Like CDs, the insurance company wants you to leave the money for the full term of the annuity. You can take it out early, but, just as with CDs, there is a penalty for early withdrawal. With annuities, this is called the surrender period, and it is usually between five and 10 years. The longer the term, the higher the surrender charge. The surrender charge may start out at 10 percent, for example, and be reduced with each passing year until it reaches zero. After that, no surrender charge exists, other than a possible tax penalty if you make withdrawals before age 59 ½.

The reason for just about any annuity is (or should be) income. With traditional fixed annuities, you may convert your annuity balance into a guaranteed income stream for just a few years or for a lifetime. Naturally, if you choose a period of years, say 10 years, you will have a higher payout than you will if you select a lifetime payout. An immediate annuity is when you opt for an income stream as soon as you purchase the annuity.

Traditional fixed annuities, or some variation of them, were the only kind available until the 1980s. The one sticking point that earned these annuities some negative press was this: Once you converted the annuity balance to an income stream, you forfeited control of the annuity. In other words, if you turned your annuity into a lifetime income stream in July, and then unexpectedly died in August, your heirs would receive nothing. The insurance company, in essence, won their bet. Had you lived to the ripe old age of 110, you would have won. That just did not sit well with the burgeoning crop of baby boomers stepping into the retirement zone, and it was one reason the insurance companies retooled annuities to accommodate changing attitudes.

Traditional fixed annuities come in two kinds: deferred (let them sit and collect interest for a while) and immediate (choose an income stream right away). The immediate annuity is sometimes called by the acronym SPIA, which stands for single premium immediate annuity.

Deferred means "postponed." With a deferred fixed annuity, taxes are not paid on gains; they are plowed back into the annuity to accelerate growth. Income is deferred down the road to allow the annuity balance to grow.

If you look at it from a problem/solution angle, when you buy life insurance you are solving the potential problem of "What if I die early?" When you buy an annuity, you are solving the potential problem of "What if I live too long?"

Fixed Indexed Annuities

Baby boomers, voting with their pocketbooks, weren't exactly snatching the old-style fixed annuities off the

shelves. They liked the idea of a guaranteed inco
pecially with pensions becoming extinct, but they ᴜᵢᷱ
like the idea of having to annuitize the contract to get it.
Annuitization means converting the annuity to an income
stream and giving up your principal. Even in the 1990s,
when the market was in an extended bull market, there
was the nagging realization that 401(k) plans, the apparent replacement for pension programs, were great if the
market continued its upward trend, but there were no
guarantees with them.

In short, the younger generation of investors, who were
now aging, wanted to have their cake and eat it too. They
wanted the guarantees of a fixed annuity, but they also
wanted the upside potential of the stock market. Sensing
this, insurance companies rolled up their sleeves in the
early 1990s, called in their actuaries and product design
people, and asked them for a solution. The result was the
fixed indexed annuity. This new indexed annuity model,
which was unveiled in 1995, would track the stock market
through an index, such as the S&P 500, and use those results at the end of each contract year to credit interest to
the contract. When the market went up, so did your balance. When the market went down, you did not participate
in those losses. Your interest locked in while you awaited
the next upturn.

There was a trade-off involved with fixed indexed annuities, or FIAs, however — you had a cap placed on your
gains. If the market index rose 30 percent in one year,
your interest earnings were capped at, say, 4 percent.
How does the name fixed indexed annuity fit this new design? They were fixed in the sense that the principal was
guaranteed. The crediting method was no longer a declared interest rate but followed a stock market index and
used its performance to determine the amount of interest

credited to the contract. And, of course, it retained its tax-deferred status and was capable, as always, of providing the annuitant with an income stream in exchange for a lump sum. You are not invested directly in the stock market, so you are immune to losses. You are "linked to" the stock market by way of the market index the company uses to credit interest to your balance each year.

Sales of FIAs shot up following the 2000 market crash and surged again after the 2008 financial crisis. Apparently, investors decided that "capped" potential, coupled with guaranteed principal, was a better way to go than all out risk with no guarantees. So, if the market crashes you can still sleep at night. Should you consider this before the next market downturn? Since Americans tend to vote for retirement products with their pocketbooks, the same way they do with cars, clothes, dog food or dish detergent, it is noteworthy that in 2013, sales of FIAs were $38.7 billion, up 16 percent from the previous year.

Crediting Strategies: When the insurance industry boosted the horsepower of the fixed indexed annuity in the 1990s, did they make it a little more complex? Yes. It reminds me of modern automobiles compared to the ones of a few decades ago. What's under the hood is much more efficient, but it's not as easy to grasp as those older engines. Once we understand how they work, however, we are that much more impressed with them.

The best way to understand how interest is credited within FIAs is to think of two buckets — a fixed interest bucket, like the old-style traditional fixed annuity, and an index bucket where the market index determines your interest credits. You can change how much you put into each bucket every year in most contracts. If you feel like the market is going to go down next year, you can move to the fixed strategy (conservative). If you feel the market will soar, move it all to the index side (aggressive). Not sure? Split it 50-50. You have nothing to lose in the market! You are not required to change it each year. Some like the set-it-and-forget-it approach. You do have several options, however, which is a good thing

A further variation on the same theme is the averaging strategy. With this strategy, the insurance company takes a "snapshot" of the market every month for 12 months. At the end of the year, the insurance company adds up the monthly results, divides by 12, and credits your account based on the average of what the market did. This type of crediting strategy works very well in a choppy market where stock prices fluctuate dramatically and often.

The monthly strategy is where the insurance company takes a snapshot of the market each month and gives you a percentage of the growth, each month standing on its own.

Why so many strategies? To confuse you? No. It is so your financial advisor can fine-tune the fixed indexed annuity to market behavior and your personal financial goals. Your advisor may recommend one strategy when the market is choppy; another when it is bullish, and yet another when a downturn is expected. You aren't going to lose money in a down market regardless of which strategy you choose, but the options give you more flexibility.

Bonuses: Insurance companies compete with banks, brokerage houses and other insurance companies for the dollars of retiring investors. To make these new products even more attractive, many companies began offering hefty bonuses. As I write this, it is not unusual to see bonuses as high as 10 percent. Let's say you deposit $100,000, and the insurance company adds a 10 percent bonus. Then your account is immediately valued at $110,000. I should note that most of these bonuses are subject to a vesting schedule, meaning that if the money is withdrawn before a contractually agreed upon date, the client will forfeit some or all of the bonus.

There are so many variations on the fixed indexed annuity that it is impossible to express them all here. To get a full rundown on all the bells and whistles, provisions, costs and limitations, work with an independent financial advisor who is also a fiduciary (works for you, not for a big company) to help you decide if a fixed indexed annuity is right for you. Work with someone who specializes in retirement income planning. They will be able to explain all of your options.

Hybrid Annuities

The term "hybrid" means two elements combined. A hybrid annuity is a fixed indexed annuity with an optional income rider attached. One metaphor I like is that of adding a sidecar to a motorcycle. You can purchase a stand-alone fixed indexed annuity, but you cannot purchase a stand-alone income rider. For the income rider to function, you must have the base annuity to go along with it. The combination has become so popular that most people who purchase index annuities (three out of four, according to www.fixedannuityfacts.com) elect to include the income rider option.

Another illustration I heard recently compared hybrid annuities to hybrid cars. A hybrid car has two engines, one gasoline-powered and the other electric.

Hybrid annuities have (1) a base account value and (2) an income account value. They each function differently, but both propel the vehicle. Both values start the same. Let's say that you deposit $200,000, and the company gives you a 10 percent bonus. With most companies, both the principal and the income base are immediately valued at $220,000. The base account value is the value of the annuity contract. This value will increase as it is credited interest based on the performance of a market index like the S&P 500. This is the value you will see in annual contract summaries; it could increase up to the annual cap — say 5 percent — or, in years that the market dips, it might be credited 0 percent. In contrast, the income account value will grow at a fixed rate outlined by your contract, sometimes called the "roll-up" rate, but is only used to calculate the value of the optional income rider. Unlike your base account value, the income account value isn't accessible in a lump sum.

When you decide to trigger the income rider, the insurance will calculate your lifetime income benefit by multiplying the income account value by a withdrawal percentage rate specified in the contract based on your age. Income withdrawals under the income rider will reduce the annuity's base account value. Also, if you withdraw more than the amount that the income rider provides, then your annual benefits will be reduced more than the total of your withdrawals. If you unexpectedly pass away after receiving only 12 months of income payments (payments may be taken in monthly increments, if desired), for example, any unused base account value will go to your designated beneficiaries. Some contracts have provisions that allow two to three times the value of your principal contract to be paid out to you over a two- or three-year period if you require long-term care.

Income Riders

When income riders were introduced in the 2000s, it was an answer to the baby boomers' aversion to annuitization (converting your contract to an income stream and forfeiting control of the account balance). Income riders also come in different shapes, sizes and names. Some are called GLWBs (guaranteed lifetime withdrawal benefits), GLIBs (guaranteed lifetime income benefits) and GLIRs (guaranteed lifetime income riders). However, they all do the same thing — provide a pension-like income in retirement. Now what do you say about holding a fixed indexed annuity inside of an IRA? Keep in mind that you are forced to take distributions at age 70 ½ if it is an IRA.

What about the cost? Income riders aren't free, but they don't cost much — between .75 percent and 1.5 percent of the fixed indexed annuity balance, annually. This cost can be expressed outright, or it can sometimes be expressed as reduced interest earnings. In other words, if the annuity earns 6 percent interest one year and the constant cost of the income rider is 75 bps (basis points), then the net return of the annuity that year would be 5.25 percent.

Guarantee

You may have noticed that acronyms for the income rider all start with the letter "G," and that the "G" stands for "guaranteed." Who guarantees the fixed indexed annuity? The insurance company that offers the annuity contract and income rider.

This boils down to the financial strength and claims-paying capability of the insurance company itself. National rating agencies such as A.M. Best, Fitch, Moody's and Standard & Poor's rate insurance companies, generally basing their ratings off of factors of the companies' financial strength. Unlike banks, insurance companies are required to hold a certain portion of their assets (set them aside) to pay out claims. These funds are required by law to be in cash or marketable securities to help ensure the insurance company has sufficient funds readily available to meet contract owners' demands. Neither annuities nor income riders are guaranteed by the FDIC.

Long-Term Care

Some, not all, insurance carriers even provide for the income to increase substantially if the fixed indexed annuity owner is confined to a nursing home or needs at-home care. Some make this coverage more expansive to include other forms of long-term care. The annuity owner typically retains access to the fixed indexed annuity's base account and continues to receive interest credits on the base account.

Roll-up Rate

A roll-up rate is the rate by which the income rider's income account value grows until the fixed indexed annuity owner triggers their income withdrawals. The income account value can have different names, including "income calculation base," "benefit base," "income benefit base" or "income account." The roll-up rate varies from carrier to carrier, but at the time this book is being written, roll-up rates are commonly between 6 and 8 percent. They tend to fluctuate with the prevailing interest rate environment. However, once the rate is locked in place (at the contract's issue date), it remains the same until the contract holder triggers their income or until the end of the roll-up period, which is typically 10 years or more. After that, the fixed indexed annuity owner may be able to extend the roll-up period at whatever rate the insurance company offers at that time.

Income

Think of the income stream like a dry river bed in front of a massive dam. The dam was constructed when you purchased the fixed indexed annuity. The lake behind the dam fills up with interest from the roll-up rate. Naturally, the longer you allow the dam untapped, the larger your lake, or your income account value, grows. You can't receive the income account value as a lump sum, but the larger it grows, the more income you can draw from your policy when you trigger your income.

Formulas for this vary from one carrier to another. Typically, if you are between the ages of 60 and 70 years of age your income may be 5 percent of your benefit base per year (paid monthly if you wish). If you start your income between the ages of 70 and 80, you may receive 6 percent of your income account value for life.

With most riders, if the accumulation value (actual account value) of the base annuity contract is higher than the income account value (calculation base), then you are able to use the higher of the two values as a calculation base. Once you trigger the income, that amount is locked in for life. Some companies have optional inflation provisions.

Remember, even as detailed as the description offered here is, it is still an overview.

CHAPTER NINE

Annuities: The Unbiased Overview

Have you ever had a prejudice? Of course you have! We all have. It means we prejudged something be- fore we knew all about it. Growing up, I completely prejudged vegetables. How could something that looked that mushy possibly taste good? I avoided vegetables for years until, you guessed it, I tasted them! Now, veggies are among my favorite foods.

Most of our prejudices are rooted in ignorance. The more we understand something, the less we fear it. Knowledge shrinks our misimpressions.

History of Annuities

The word "annuity" comes from the Latin word, annus, which means yearly. The Latin word annua meant "a system of annual payments." We get our English words "annual" and "anniversary" from the same root. Nothing too scary about that. A fixed indexed annuity is no more than a contract purchased by an individual from an insurance company. Annuities are commonly used to secure a retirement income in fixed payments over a set period. Nothing scary about that, is there? So far, so good?

The concept of the fixed annuity as a financial instrument got its start back in the days of ancient Rome as mentioned before.

The use of annuities all but died out during the Dark Ages but was revived in London, England, when people like Edmund Halley (of Halley's Comet fame) began tinkering with mortality tables and life expectancy figures.[42]

Annuities Come to America

Annuities on American soil began with the Presbyterian Ministers Fund, founded in Philadelphia, Pennsylvania, in 1759. It started out as a church-sponsored relief fund for widows and children of Presbyterian ministers and later became a commercial enterprise. Benjamin Franklin understood the power of compounding interest in annuities. According to The Actuary Magazine, he left the city of Boston a fixed annuity in his will that continued to pay out until the early 1990s, and only stopped because the city

---

[42] Edwin W. Kopf. Casact.org. "The Early History of the Annuity." https://www.casact.org/pubs/proceed/proceed26/26225.pdf. Accessed Nov. 18, 2016.

elected to take a lump-sum payout of the remaining balance.[43]

During the American Civil War, 1861-1865, the Union government borrowed a page from the Romans and used annuities instead of land grants to compensate soldiers. President Abraham Lincoln endorsed a plan using annuities to help widows and families of disabled veterans.[44]

In 1929, when the U.S. stock market collapsed, and bank failures became commonplace, annuities were seen as safe havens for cash and annuities became a staple of the insurance landscape. TIAA-CREF offered the first variable deferred annuity in 1952 and tax reform strengthened the annuity market in 1986. In the 1990s, annuities got a major facelift and with the introduction of the fixed indexed annuity in 1995 and riders that made it possible to receive a guaranteed lifetime income without annuitizing the contract.[45]

A Word About the Media

On the financial channels (and there must be at least a dozen of them on our cable service), one market analyst comes on and gives an expert opinion about a particular stock, or the general direction the economy is heading. Following a commercial break, another talking head comes on and offers an opinion diametrically opposed to the first one but equal in certainty. The producers of these

---

[43] Joe Halpern and Greg Henke. The Actuary. April/May, 2014. "Structured-Note Annuity: A Niche Industry is Born With Endless Possibilities." https://www.soa.org/ Library/Newsletters/The-Actuary-Magazine/2014/april/act-2014-vol11-iss2-toc.aspx. Accessed Nov. 18, 2016.

[44] Mark P. Cussen. Investopedia. 2011. "Introduction to Annuities: The History of Annuities." http://www.investopedia.com/university/annuities/#ixzz4OOliJkBh. Accessed Nov. 18, 2016.

[45] Ibid.

shows must be convinced that it makes for great television, but it comes across as a shade above professional wrestling as far as believability is concerned. I am sure it is perplexing to anyone seeking honest-to-goodness information.

One such channel parades onto the set a stock market "guru" to give his "expert" opinion. He does this in such a clownish way that we are left scratching our heads, "Is this guy for real?" It is a call-in show, but they must screen the calls well, because no one ever bothers to ask him why he wears funny hats, rings cowbells and squeezes a bulb horn to punctuate his opinions. Really? It would be good comedy if it were not for the fact that the "stock-picking guru" gives buy and sell recommendations, and people actually take his advice. When naïve investors act on his stock picks with their hard-earned money and then lose it, "Mr. Funny Hat" is safely off the air and bears no responsibility whatsoever.

One of his more famous gaffes took place on a March 8, 2008, show. A viewer had written in to ask: "Should I be worried about Bear Stearns in terms of liquidity and get my money out of there?" The self-proclaimed stock prophet with the rolled up shirt sleeves screamed into the microphone, "No, No, NO! Bear Stearns is fine! Do not take your money out! This is ridiculous! Don't be silly!" Six days later, Bear Stearns, one of the mega-banks that caused the financial meltdown of 2008, was on hands and knees begging for a government bailout after its stock had plummeted 90 percent, virtually overnight.

When I fly, I usually pass by at least a dozen newsstands on my way to the gate. I am always amazed at how many financial magazines are in print these days. Like the financial cable channels, these periodicals seem to thrive on controversy and flat-out sensational pronouncements.

In one newsstand rack, I saw an entire row of magazines on finance, some with titles I recognized, such as Money, Barron's and Kiplinger's. There were several others I had not seen before, all with headlines competing for attention:

- "Buy Gold NOW!"
- "Don't Buy Gold!"
- "10 Hot Stock Tips!" (I personally will never call you with a hot stock tip.)

Somewhere along the line, the media seem to have lost the part of its compass that points north. The people responsible for publishing these magazines and the folks who produce these television shows must have all come to the conclusion that we, the gullible public, have low IQs and short attention spans. They must think that we have to be fed short sound bites and shocking headlines, or we will lose our concentration. Personally, I would settle for straight facts and unbiased reporting — rare these days.

Annuities in the Media

Financial magazines often give blanket advice and make broad assumptions where the bias is thinly veiled. To find out why this is, all you have to do is look at the advertisements on the pages between the articles. Follow the money trail. Advertisers pay the printing bills, and anyone who thinks advertising dollars do not influence editorial content is naïve. Product promotion is nothing new in the entertainment industry. In the movie "E.T. the Extraterrestrial," you probably remember the kid luring the E.T. out of hiding by dropping Reese's Pieces. With the close-up shots of the bag and multiple mentions of the product in the dialogue, how could you miss it? The story goes that Hershey's paid the producers of the film $1 million for that. Mars, makers of M&Ms, passed up on the deal. It is no accident that James Bond is shown driving a BMW in one film instead of the Aston Martin DB5 as was called for in the original screenplay. I have no problem with such obvious product placement in entertainment, but it is reprehensible for advertising dollars to bias editorial content disguised as hard news.

Stories that attack annuities and other insurance-based products are most common in magazines supported by the advertising dollars of brokerage houses. No surprise, right? The economic meltdown of 2008 gave investors a taste of how dangerous a place the stock market could be, especially for their retirement money. When millions of Americans went running to the safety and guaranteed growth of annuities, the stockbrokers' claws came out, and some of the worst propaganda against annuities started to appear in print. Ironically, many who had turned to the safety of annuities were whistling a happy tune while many stockbrokers were letting their telephone calls go to message machines.

Let me set the record straight on something. I am by no means preaching a sermon on the virtues of annuities, any more than I am blasting the stock market. Both have their place in the great financial scheme of things. To boil it down to its essence, I am for truth and against lies. I would take up the same sword in defense of any other person, place or thing I thought was being arbitrarily demonized in the media purely for profit motives. To their credit, some of the die-hard columnists seem to be peering past the propaganda curtain. The key is using the right tool for the job — just like using the hammer instead of a screwdriver with my grandfather when I was a kid. I recommend that my clients separate their money for basic living expenses from their fun money. Protect what is essential to live on and have fun with the rest.

Jane Bryant Quinn, the revered financial columnist for the Washington Post, used to maintain a hard and fast stance against all annuities. In 2010, however, she wrote a surprising article entitled, "Set Up a Future Income With New-Style Annuities." She said, "Praise for these contracts is surprising, coming from me ... But for people without pensions, the guarantees themselves are attractive, despite the fees. In fact, they're more generous than they should be."[46]

What changed her mind? Annuities had changed, and she noticed it.

The Wharton Report

There used to be a television commercial back in the 1980s about E.F. Hutton. The camera pans across a noisy dinner party and then zooms in on two men at the table. One man leans over and says to the other man, "Well, my broker is E.F. Hutton and..." He does not finish his sentence because the room instantly falls silent. The other guests lean forward, their hands cupped around their ears, straining to hear what E.F. Hutton's advice was. The commercial finished with a deep voice saying off camera, "When E.F. Hutton talks ... people listen."

I remember seeing the commercial as a teenager and wondering who in the heck E.F. Hutton was. He must be one smart individual to cause that kind of reaction. I would learn later that it was Edward Francis Hutton, who started the brokerage house in 1904 (thus the name) and that in 1988, it would be gobbled up by one of its Wall Street competitors.

---

[46] Jane Quinn. CBS Money Watch. June 4, 2010. "Set Up a Future Retirement Income, with New-Style Annuities."
http://www.cbsnews.com/news/set-up-a-future-retirement-income-with-new-style-annuities/. Accessed Nov. 18, 2016.

The Wharton Financial Institutions Center has that sort of prestige in the world of economic analysis today, particularly in the area of personal finance.

Professors Craig B. Merrill and Professor David F. Babbel, are to 21st century retirement income planning what Wernher von Braun and company were to aerospace engineering during the space race. The Wharton School of the University of Pennsylvania is globally recognized for intellectual leadership in all things financial. Professors Merril and Babbel published an independent research paper in 2010 known as the "Wharton Report," or "Real World Index Annuity Returns," that compared the returns of indexed annuities with those of the stock market. This favorable comment appeared on page nine of the report: "for moderate and strongly risk-averse individuals, the fixed indexed annuity is judged superior in performance to various combinations of stocks and bonds."[47]

Another independent research paper published by Professors Merril and Babbel included the following favorable comments about annuities: "In the case of life annuities, the risk of outliving one's income is pooled among all annuity purchases, providing a kind of insurance against outliving one's assets."

They describe the fixed indexed annuity as "the only investment vehicle that allows its owners an income to "spend at the same rate, but be covered for as long as they live."[48]

---

[47] David F. Babbel, Geoffrey VanderPal and Jack Marrion. Wharton University of Pennsylvania. Dec. 27, 2010. "Real World Index Annuity Returns." https://papers.ssrn. com/sol3/papers.cfm?abstract_id=1482023. Accessed Nov. 18, 2016.

[48] David F. Babbel and Craig B. Merrill. Wharton Financial Institutions Center. Aug. 14, 2007. "Policy Brief: Personal Finance, Investing your Lump Sum at Retirement." http://www.slideshare.net/bryandaly/wharton-study-onincomeannuities-1. Accessed Nov. 18, 2016.

What makes the comments of these two members of the academic community significant is that they have no stake, no profit motive, no axe to grind and no grudge to bear. They are, in other words, unbiased. To my knowledge, neither Professor Merrill nor Professor Babbel sells annuities. Neither does the Government Accountability Office (GAO), an investigative arm of Congress charged with examining matters relating to the receipt and payment of public funds. Their stated agenda is to help shed light on solutions to problems facing retirees. In a July, 2010 report, they addressed the projected problem of too many seniors running out of money in retirement. Their recommendation, put very plainly, was to "delay taking Social Security and buy a fixed indexed annuity."

"The risk that retirees will outlive their assets is a growing challenge," said the GAO report, adding that almost half of those nearing retirement will run out of money and will not be able to cover basic expenses and uninsured health care costs. An annuity can protect retirees from the risk of outliving their savings, the study said.[49]

The Truth Is Usually in the Middle

There is a natural divide in the financial planning world. On the one side are stockbrokers who earn their living selling stocks, bonds and mutual funds, and on the other side are insurance people who make their living selling insurance solutions.

If you were to come suddenly into a sum of money, say $300,000, you have to put it somewhere, right? If you walk into one of these large brokerage houses and ask to

---

[49] Temma Ehrenfeld. Financial Planning. July 1, 2011. "GAO Recommends Retirees Invest in Annuities, Delay Taking Social Security." http://www.financial-planning.com/news/gao-recommends-retirees-invest-in-annuities-delay-taking-social-security. Accessed Nov. 18, 2016.

speak to a financial advisor, what advice do you expect to receive? They will likely show you a menu of sorts.

"Let's see... we should diversify by putting some in large cap stocks, some in small cap stocks, a little in international funds, some in stocks and a small amount in money market in case you need quick access to it."

If you take the same $300,000 to an insurance agent who sells annuities, guess what? They will find an insurance-based solution for every bit of your money. The same would be true if you took the $300,000 problem to a real estate professional. He or she would probably have just the property that would give you a nice return on your investment.

There are two sides to every coin, and the truth is usually in the middle. The CPA in me impels me to look at financial problem-solving from 30,000 feet up. What is the overall objective of the person sitting across from me? What do they want to do with their money? That is why I spend most of the hour in my consultations with people asking lots of questions. What do you want to do in retirement? Why do you have your money invested as you do? When do you wish to retire? How much money will you need when you do?

I have concluded that annuities have their place. They are not the be-all and end-all, but there is a place for them in a balanced portfolio, especially for retirees seeking to guarantee a portion of their income. This is particularly true for retirees who will need additional income to cover their living expenses if their pension (assuming they have one) and their Social Security do not cover their essential monthly expenses.

Fiduciary Responsibility

Fiduciary is a word we do not use every day, but it is an important one if you are seeking advice on investments. The English word "fiduciary" comes from the Latin word which means "holding in trust." Cousin words are "fidelity" and "confidence," which share the same root.

In legal terms, a fiduciary is someone who is sworn to act in the interests of his or her clients, putting all personal interests aside. Fiduciaries are legally bound to be loyal to their clients and can lose their license and their livelihood if they are not. Can a fiduciary profit from a transaction? Of course. But they must not profit from a transaction at the expense of their client's best interest.

For example, I act in a fiduciary capacity with all of my clients. I could never fulfill that role if I worked for one company or a group of companies. Most stockbrokers deal exclusively in stocks and bonds, and their training and certification is restricted to the world of equities and market trading. They will naturally be cool to the idea of offering financial planning tools offered by insurance companies. They know little about them and will probably have a bias against them. Since they don't receive their income from that corner of the financial planning world, they will have little interest in the financial planning solutions they offer.

The same goes for insurance agents whose education, certification and affiliations limit them to offering only insurance products. They will likely have a jaundiced view of the stock market and see only its negative aspects.

A fiduciary's toolbox will contain tools of all sorts and he or she will not be married to any of them. The tool or strategy a fiduciary will select in structuring a financial plan will be the right one for the job. A fiduciary will not attempt to build a plan around a product or strategy. A fiduciary will have blinders on, so to speak. Fiduciaries do not work for any one brokerage house or insurance carrier. They are independent. They work exclusively for the client. It is not unusual for a financial plan drawn up by a true fiduciary to include both equity strategies and insurance strategies along with other investment and income concepts if that is what it takes to ensure a sensible and productive asset picture.

One of my favorite quotes on this is by Abraham Maslow, who said, "If all you have is a hammer, everything looks like a nail."

CHAPTER TEN

The Advantages of Holistic Planning

What does the word "holistic" mean? It comes from the word "whole" and it means to consider the whole problem, person or situation when rendering help, issuing advice or recommending medical treatment.

In medicine, for example, a holistic physician would not just treat the symptom. A holistic doctor would take into consideration all the human systems that might be causing the symptom to exist — physical, social, spiritual, emotional and psychological.

For example, if a 65-year-old woman comes in complaining of knee pain, it would be easy just to write her a prescription for painkillers and let it go at that. It might make the pain go away temporarily, but would it really solve the woman's problem? The holistic approach would require asking the woman questions to get to the root of the issue. If the doctor does this, he or she will find that the woman lost her husband a few years ago and began to suffer bouts of depression. She now lives alone. She is an emotional eater. The depression and the loneliness have caused her to gain weight. On top of that, she has had to take on a part-time job that requires her to stand on her feet all day. Further tests reveal that she has developed Type 2 diabetes and hypertension. The holistic physician may indeed prescribe pain medicine for her knee but will also realize the root of her problem is situational and psychological. The holistic medical approach might start with her depression and then move to helping her improve her diet. This would take pressure off the knee and allow her to exercise more. This, in turn, would result in an overall improvement in the woman's health because the whole individual was treated, not just a knee.

In other cases, lack of proper sleep can cause depression. Depression can actually increase the body's sensitivity to pain. Parts of the body that wouldn't hurt otherwise now become painful. The holistic medical approach would be to find out what's making the patient not sleep. I know of one case where the cure for sleeplessness lay in getting an hour of exercise per day and drinking more water. No pills needed. But it started with asking questions.

Holistic Financial Planning

Remember Scrooge McDuck, the Disney cartoon character of our childhood? He was the billionaire uncle of Donald Duck, who was so in love with his money that his favorite thing was to splash around in his "money bin," a roomful of coins and cash. Even as kids we knew that Scrooge McDuck was nuts. He should have done something purposeful with his money, not wallow in it.

When we look at the big picture, money is no more than numbers on paper until it has a purpose. Job number one of the holistic financial planner is to determine what that purpose is. What do you want to do with your money? What are your life goals? What is important to you?

Some people start that planning process with clearly defined specific goals. They know exactly how much they need to have in the way of income in order to live their desired lifestyle in retirement. They have a crystal-clear view of their financial future and can readily articulate their short-term and long-range goals. They are in the minority, however. Most folks need a little help in clearly defining their future financially.

The expression "different strokes for different folks" definitely applies here. As we mentioned earlier in this book, there is no one-size-fits-all, and there are no cookie-cutter solutions with holistic financial planning. Life goals are as varied and individual as fingerprints. Some are determined to leave a sterling legacy for their children and grandchildren and others are not. Some have their heart set on travel when they retire, while for others the ideal retirement scenario involves staying at home, spending time with family. Still others have a passion they wish to pursue. It could be golf or a second career. The lists are endless. Holistic planning is working toward those life goals through proper management of resources.

From the planner's point of view, the process starts with asking many questions to gather information. The objective is not necessarily a number, although numbers will definitely enter into the picture. The objective is to help the client identify and realize his or her life goals. The holistic process will involve determining where the client's current resources are and why they are there — making sure the management and disposition of the individual's assets matches up with his or her life goals.

Before holistic financial planners can make recommendations, they need to examine such areas as risk tolerance, lifestyle preferences, taxes, estate documents, assets and resources, insurance and income. Taking a holistic approach they will do all of this within the context of the big picture, not on one single financial issue. A qualified planner may work with you on a single financial issue but within the context of your overall situation.

Holistic Planning Step-by-Step

1. Clearly defining the financial advisor-client relationship: I put this first because it is first. Clients have the right to know what is expected from their financial advisor and what planning and investment philosophy he or she adheres to. Is the financial advisor a fiduciary — someone who is bound by oath to work solely in the best interests of the client, and not motivated by profit? How will the financial advisor be paid? What are the financial advisor's credentials? All of this needs to be defined, and the client's questions about such matters answered in the initial consultation. I like to put it this way: "Let's see if it is a fit that you and I work together first." After that is established, we can roll up our sleeves and get to work.

2. Obtaining all the facts: As Yogi Berra said, "If you don't know where you are going you might not get there." (Think about it.) This is where we identify financial goals and establish timelines. This is the time to gather data relevant to the financial planning process, such as account information and documents pertaining to the estate. I call this "taking the snapshot" of the client's financial world.

Where clients have positioned their assets may or may not match their stated goals.

3. Analysis and Evaluation: This usually takes place between the first and second meeting of the financial advisor and client. It takes time to analyze the accounts, determine if they are performing according to the client's wishes and stated goals. The adage, "if it ain't broke, don't fix it" applies here. But if the current situation doesn't match the client's goals, this is where repair recommendations are formulated and discussed at the next meeting. The financial advisor must compare assets with liabilities, look at cash flow and insurance coverage, examine all estate documents, review tax strategies and analyze investments.

4. Presenting recommendations: With the "big picture" now in clear focus and the smaller elements that make it up clearly identified, this is where the financial advisor gives the findings of his or her analysis to the client and makes recommendations. These recommendations are carefully thought out suggestions and are open to discussion. Nothing is cast in concrete. A competent physician always makes sure the patient completely and thoroughly understands any medicine or procedure. Likewise, the holistic financial advisor answers every question to the complete satisfaction of the client. The client must understand each and every strategy the financial advisor recommends and feel comfortable with them beyond doubt. Client feedback is invited and welcomed and recommendations are tweaked as necessary here.

5. Implementation: When everyone involved is comfortable and on the same page, then the client and financial advisor can agree on how and when the recommendations will be carried out. The ball is entirely in the client's court at this point. The client, not the financial advisor, pushes the "go" button on any course of action that has been discussed. After all, it is the client's money and the client's ultimate decision. The client should never feel pressured or harried and should never make a decision rashly. This is where the process may involve other professionals who have been working behind the scenes, such as tax professionals, accountants or attorneys.

6. Periodic review and monitoring: The financial advisor is a financial coach. One can't imagine the coach laying out the game plan and then leaving the players on the field to fend for themselves. Holistic financial advisors will monitor their clients' progress toward their stated goals. The financial advisor will report to the client on at least an annual basis, if not more often, to review the plan. Are the strategies in place still the best options? Are the client's goals still being met? Does the client have questions? Are changes needed in any elements of the plan?

As the process of holistic planning unfolds, it quickly becomes apparent that all areas of an individual's financial life are intertwined. The small decisions comprise a mosaic of the whole.

What Holistic Financial Planning ISN'T

Here is what holistic financial planning is not: A couple, both age 65, thumb through the yellow pages looking for a "financial advisor." They find the address of the local office of "Big Stocks Brokerage Company." They arrive at the address and find the office of BSBC is in a tall, glass and steel building, indicating, of course that these people must know what they are doing. When they ask to see a financial advisor, they are escorted through double glass doors and over to an agent who works for Big Stocks Brokerage Company. The couple explains that they are ready to retire, and they would like to deposit their life's savings of $500,000 with Big Stocks Brokerage Company and let them handle their financial affairs.

What do you think will happen here? The "financial advisor" will likely turn a computer screen toward the couple with the following selections:

- Conservative
- Moderately conservative
- Moderate
- Moderately aggressive
- Aggressive

All of these choices, by the way, are stock market investments of one kind or another.

"Which best suits your risk profile?" asks the "financial advisor."

The husband and wife exchange glances and whispers and land on the middle one.

"Moderate!" says the wife.

"Yes. Moderate," echoes the husband.

The "financial advisor" moves the cursor to the "moderate" icon and clicks the mouse. The screen changes to a colorful image of a pie chart, indicating where the couple's $500,000 will be invested:

- 35% large company stocks
- 10% small company stocks
- 15% international stocks
- 35% fixed income
- 5% cash (money market)

"What about safety?" they ask.

"Safety? No worries!" replies the "financial advisor." "The market has always gone up and down over the years, but going all the way back to 1970 it has averaged 9.8 percent!"

To ease their minds, the "financial advisor" hands them a thick book with many pages of colorful graphs and charts that show the historical performance of "moderate" portfolios. The projections point to a rosy outcome. I have noticed a trend in my conversations with seniors about income planning for retirement. More and more of them are interested, not in projections, but guarantees. Not only guarantees, but because people are living longer, they are interested — now more than ever — in lifetime guarantees. They seem to want assurances (not hazy predictions) when it comes to their future income.

Financial Advisors

In the above scenario, you probably noticed that I put quotes around "financial advisor." Anyone can hang out a shingle and call him- or herself a financial advisor. We are a free market society, and "financial advisor," or "financial adviser" (the spellings are interchangeable) is not a legal designation. It is simply a term denoting someone who provides financial advice. In Chapter Nine of this book, I went into considerable detail about the term "fiduciary." Not all "financial advisors" are obligated to offer advice that is 100 percent in the best interest of their clients. Some financial advisors could not do so even if they wanted to. Why? Because they work for a company or corporation that expects them to offer their products and services exclusively. In the above scenario, the agent of Big Stocks is limited to the products and services marketed by Big Stocks and works with a limited toolbox when it comes to overall financial planning.

Think of it this way. If you are in the market for a new automobile and you walk into a Ford dealership, do you think the salesperson will tell you that Chevy has the better product? I doubt it. They work for Ford.

When seeking financial advice, if you consult with an insurance agent you are likely to get insurance solutions. No surprise there. If you consult with stockbrokers, you are likely to get only market-based solutions. No surprise there. The only way to get unbiased solutions that are not influenced by remuneration or profit motive is to consult with a fiduciary who is legally bound and obligated by moral and ethical standards to offer only advice that is in the best interests of the client and is dually licensed to sell both securities and insurance.

In the next chapter, we will explore how to select the right financial advisor. There is more to it than just plucking a name off the Internet or picking a firm out of the yellow pages.

CHAPTER ELEVEN

Finding the Right Financial Advisor for You

Two areas of life in which I strongly encourage you not to procrastinate or take a do-it-yourself approach are your health and your wealth. I personally know of individuals who would use any excuse to wiggle out of seeing a doctor for an annual physical. "That's just the way I roll," said one man who is no longer with us. His modus operandi was to wait until he had a pain that could not be dismissed by Tylenol or aspirin and then, maybe, after a few days of it, he might go seek medical attention. Sure enough, this time the pain was from an inoperable malignant tumor. If he had dealt with the problem earlier, his death could have been prevented.

I know of no one who would attempt self-surgery or self-dentistry, but there are plenty who take a do-it-yourself approach to managing their wealth. I am not talking about recreational stock trading, or what I call "incidental investing." I have some beloved clients who enjoy using discretionary funds to trade in the stock market. The key word here is discretionary. In other words, they are using money they can afford to lose — money they have set aside for that purpose. They are not pumping their life's savings or, even worse, borrowed money, into these online trades. Some of these individuals have become quite adept at technical analysis and have learned how to maneuver in and out of positions. Their accounts are in the positive, and they have done well. The other side of the coin, however, is that some have failed miserably at it and don't know when to back away from the computer.

I remember seeing a cartoon after the tech bubble burst in 2000. It depicted a sad-faced man standing on a street corner, dressed in a tattered business suit, holding up a hand-lettered sign that read: "Need Money to Continue Day Trading." Online trading has an appeal similar to the lights and sounds of Las Vegas, and millions of Americans have lost millions of dollars to its lure.

I am not so much talking about online trading as I am overall financial management. I am talking about taking a do-it-yourself approach to the placement of assets for income in that all-important phase of life when income is critically important — retirement. Most people make expensive mistakes that a competent, experienced financial expert could have helped them avoid.

Emotional Decisions

Some fall into the trap of letting their emotions get in the way. They buy hot stock picks based on tips, rumors or the advice of friends and have difficulty letting go when these investments falter. This is easier to do that you may think. I know of some who invested heavily in the company they worked for and were bitterly disappointed. Take Nortel, for example, a telecommunications giant of the 1990s, which at one time boasted of $30 billion in annual revenue and employed almost 100,000 people worldwide. I know of some Nortel employees who, because they worked there, loaded up company stock when it was $40 per share. When it doubled, they were ecstatic and put every dime they could muster into it. They were on cloud nine in July 2000 when the share price peaked at $124.50. Within two years, however, Nortel was approaching bankruptcy and the stock was worth pennies per share. For some, the fall of Nortel was merely a headline on the financial page, but for those who had bet their life's savings it was financial ruin.

Investment Noise

Some chase the next Google or Apple, which is a little like playing the lottery. Others, wishing to play it safe, go all in with mutual funds, only to have their earnings diminished by exorbitant fees. Still others are just plain confused by the noise of conflicting advice spewed on a daily basis by the media, both print and electronic. There are so many investment vehicles out there. Where should they have their money? Bonds? Annuities? Exchange-traded funds? Real estate investment trusts? Cash value life insurance? You can't trust the press. Too many of the articles are written by brokers and agents who earn commissions selling the products they are touting, and there is a new one every week.

Tax Considerations

As a tax professional, I can tell you that one of the biggest mistakes made by those who go it alone is failure to see the tax consequences of their investment decisions until it is too late. By "too late," I mean when the IRS comes calling for their share. The website www.IRS.gov puts the word count of the IRS Code at 3.7 million. That's more words than the Holy Bible (788,280), "War and Peace" (560,000), and the windy L. Ron Hubbard's science fiction satire, "An Alien Affair," which weighs in at 1.2 million words, combined. Even the government acknowledges that the tax code is ridiculously complex. Since the rules change on a yearly basis, complying with the tax code is like shooting at a moving target. That still does not mean you can get a pass from the IRS by writing, "I didn't understand" on your noncompliant tax return. If you are audited, you will still pay the taxes, and, more often than not, a penalty.

As you advance across the years, drawing your own personal timeline, you will encounter several intersections where your financial future will be impacted by the decisions you make or fail to make — marriage, employment, children, retirement. Making the wrong decision, or making no decision at all, could cost you financially to the tune of years of lost earnings, unnecessary taxes or missed opportunities.

I hope I have made the case for seeking professional help when it comes to managing your assets, especially as you near the threshold of retirement. But that leaves the question we came here to address unanswered. How do you go about selecting the right financial advisor for your unique and special circumstances?

Selecting the Right Financial Advisor

I like the interview process for this one. If you are going to place your trust, confidence and life's savings into someone's hands, don't you think it is a good idea to know them both personally and professionally? I do. True professionals will feel the same way. They will not mind your asking questions about their credentials and qualifications. They will welcome your inquiries. They will be happy to tell you about their training and the designations they have earned that represent their expertise and experience. The term "financial advisor" varies state by state, so make sure you are dealing with a fiduciary.

Let's call the individual you are considering as your personal financial advisor the "candidate." Take a look at the candidate's office walls. This is not a perfect indicator of their professional qualifications. Not all professionals put plaques and certificates on the wall, but most of them do.

Check out the candidate's business card. This is also not a perfect indicator of the candidate's credentials. Not all professionals put their certifications and designations on their business card, but most of them do. Do the letters after his or her name look like alphabet soup to you? Ask what the letters mean. If you don't understand each one, ask again until you understand.

A competent, qualified professional will not mind this little interrogation. After all, trust is a big factor in this undertaking. You may be deciding who will guide you through some of the most crucial money decisions of your life. Your life's savings may be involved. It is one thing to hang out a shingle that proclaims to the world that you are a "financial advisor" and it is quite another to prove by evidence that you have spent years obtaining the required education it takes to render such advice accurately and effectively.

If you have ever been traveling and asked directions, you probably know what it feels like to be given wrong directions. The individual who provided the wrong turn may not have done it maliciously, but that does not make the wasted time and misdirection any less painful. Similarly, with your finances, following errant advice can cost you thousands of dollars that represent years of hard work and diligent saving.

Designations and Certifications

Here is the thing about all those letters you may or may not see after the candidate's name on his or her business card or office wall. They mean nothing in and of themselves. The implied knowledge, wisdom, experience and competence they represent are what is important. Sometimes this has to boil down to your impressions of the candidate's responses to your questions. When asked a question, does the candidate fumble and mumble with the answer, or is the answer forthright and on point? That one is up to you.

With that little disclaimer in place, however, here is a list of designations you may see attached to the name of the financial advisor candidate and what they mean. You may not see all of them. Professionals specialize, you know. Nevertheless, you could expect to see at least one or two of them.[50]

---

[50] RiA Stands for you. "Interview Questions to Ask Advisors." http://www.riastands foryou.com/choosing-an-advisor.html. Accessed Nov. 18, 2016.

- CFP® professionals, also known as CERTIFIED FINANCIAL PLANNER™ professionals: A CFP® professional has completed university-level financial planning coursework and passed a 10-hour exam covering nearly 90 topics, from group medical insurance to derivatives.
- CPA® (Certified Public Accountant): an accountant who has passed certain examinations and met all other statutory and licensing requirements of a United States state to be certified by that state.
- ChFC® (Chartered Financial Consultant): The ChFC® designation was introduced in 1982 as an alternative to the CFP®. It has the same core curriculum as the CFP® board certification, plus a couple of additional courses, but does not require a comprehensive board exam.
- Investment Advisor Representative: Although not a designation, Investment Advisor Representatives are required by law to uphold the highest level of commitment in serving the client's best interest. They are subject to state regulators auditing their practice at any time. The costs, legal responsibilities and additional oversight associated with taking on this duty mean that few financial professionals actually become registered as Investment Advisor Representatives.

That is by no means all of the designations and certifications out there, and I am certainly not endorsing any one of them as the centerpiece of the crown jewels of credentials. Some certifications are issued by the state, others by educational facilities and still others by the regulatory arms of the industry (or profession) itself, just as the medical profession provides certification to its members in certain fields.

Designations and certifications are important, but education and experience are vital. Which surgeon would you prefer work on you? One who had every degree and certificate in the book, or one who had successfully performed identical operations on hundreds if not thousands of patients over the years? I thought so. That's why I always grade on the curve when it comes to credentials, giving more points to years of experience, solid reputation and the good recommendation of satisfied clients than to letters after a name on the business card.

Ask Questions

When you interview a candidate to fill your financial advisory position, here are some questions you may wish to ask.

How are you paid? You aren't asking for their bank balance or net worth. You just want to know if there are any possible conflicts of interests. How financial advisors are paid may reveal the level of their objectivity when it comes to their recommendations.

No financial advisor works free of charge. Companies that market financial products compete for your business just like any other sector of the American economy. They are willing to pay commissions. True fiduciaries are never under an obligation to recommend any one product or service, however. They are required to maintain their independence so they can make recommendations irrespective of commissions.

Anyone who has ever used a travel agency has benefited by commissions. When you book a flight or plan a vacation through a travel agency, you expect them to save you money and improve the quality of your trip — yet you never pay them a dime! A travel agency can shop for the best fares and accommodations for you. As part of their service, they will ascertain what is important to you on your trip. Your itinerary will be tailor-made to your preferences. So who pays them? They are compensated by the ultimate provider of the services. There's nothing wrong with that as long as you, the client, are the ultimate benefactor. What would be wrong, however, would be if you flew on a noncompetitive airline or stayed in a substandard hotel because the travel agent was more interested in making money than seeing to it that your best interests were cared for.

What is your investment philosophy? Pay attention to the answer to this question. True professionals will not answer this question until they know what you want your assets to accomplish for you. It's like asking a taxi driver "Where are you headed?" That's the question they should be asking you! Their professional purpose (that of the financial advisor, I mean) should be to get you where you want to go. The true professional will ask you questions about your time horizon, your risk tolerance, your income needs, your current holdings, your tax situation and many others. Can you imagine a doctor prescribing medicine before giving you a thorough examination and determining whether you are allergic to it? Of course not! A professional financial advisor will be very interested in what you have to say and will not make recommendations without a full and thorough financial "examination."

If the answer to, "What is your investment philosophy?" begins with a list of stocks, bonds and mutual funds that are projected to return a stated amount over the next 10 years, you are probably talking to an accumulation specialist, not a retirement income specialist. You may consider looking elsewhere for advice if you are on the threshold of retirement. It's like a 40-year-old visiting a pediatrician for a health issue. They are probably a competent physician in their field, but maybe not right for you.

How will we work together? Before you decide to work with a financial advisor, there are a few "housekeeping" items that need to be aired out. Who will your contact person be, and how often will they review your financial plan with you? Your first meeting will likely be with the firm's principal. Who will actually manage your portfolio? A financial plan is a living, breathing thing. Times change. Tax rules change. Your life will change. Your holdings will increase. Doesn't it make sense that you have a regular conference with the people who are watching over your finances, at least annually? I certainly do.

Good communication between you and your financial advisory team is crucial. Some people place a greater value on personal rapport than others. From time to time, we interview people who tell us they have been with a financial advisor for several years. They know the person and trust them. Sometimes they are like a member of the family.

All that is good. I would like to think most of my clients feel that way about me. More important, however, is what you know about your financial advisor professionally. Do they have fiduciary responsibility? Do they report directly to you or to a company? Do you know how they are compensated? What if your financial advisor only receives compensation when he or she makes changes to your portfolio? Could that possibly result in too many trades? Could profit motive enter into their decisions regarding your portfolio? These are professional questions, not personal ones, and you need answers that are detailed and to your complete satisfaction.

Other Qualifiers

Does your candidate for financial advisor understand taxes? Can they address this most important area of financial planning? I once saw a quote that went like this: "It's not how much you make, it's how much you get to keep that matters." Taxes can have an enormous impact on us in retirement. Most people I interview are perfectly willing to pay their fair share of taxes, but they don't want to pay one penny more than their fair share, and I don't blame them.

The tax code is voluminous and complex, but there are many provisions that are hiding in plain sight. If your financial advisor knows where to find them and put them into action for you, you can reduce, and in many cases eliminate, thousands of dollars in taxes each year.

When you are choosing a financial advisor, ask all the questions you know to ask about taxes, and then ask if there are any questions you forgot to ask. A financial advisor who is an expert in taxes will usually point out several more.

One area often missed by financial advisors is individual retirement accounts, or IRAs. A competent financial advisor will educate clients on strategies designed to prevent a client from making Uncle Sam the IRAs biggest beneficiary. A competent financial advisor will always pay particular attention to the "designated beneficiary form." The way IRAs work, if the client doesn't use up all the money in retirement, it goes to heirs. How that transfer takes place is critical. A qualified tax professional can "stretch" the IRA to multiple generations (sometimes called a "multi-gen" IRA) and pass the wealth onto children and grandchildren with minimal tax obligations. Because of the power of compounding, this strategy often substantially increases the inheritance to heirs over time.

Do they understand insurance? Competent financial advisors will not "sell" insurance to clients if they don't need it, but they also will not ignore the value that insurance can have to their clients, especially to those who are retiring. Competent financial advisors will know just how much insurance has changed in the last 10 to 15 years and understand how to put some of those changes to work for their clients. For example, sophisticated life insurance strategies exist that may allow clients to avoid unnecessary taxation when it comes to their IRAs.

Let's say a client owns an IRA but does not need income from the IRA in retirement. When they turn 70 ½, they will be forced to take their required minimum distribution (RMD). If they qualify, they may use those RMDs to pay premiums on a life insurance policy with a face amount equal to the amount of the IRA. That way, they pass the value of the IRA to their heirs completely tax free! This strategy was perfect for one client who, when he turned 70 ½ was angry when he learned that he would be forced to withdraw money from his IRAs (he had several) even though he did not need the income. When he learned he could leverage those RMDs into a life insurance policy that passes the full value of those accounts to his loved ones tax-free, he was ecstatic. In fact, when we ran the numbers, if he lived another 10 years he would be able to leave them double what his IRAs would have been worth.

Long-term care insurance is a conundrum for some. Insurance costs for nursing homes and assisted living facilities can be so costly that it is practically beyond reach. Not only are the premiums expensive, but it's like car insurance — if you don't use it, the premiums are gone forever. Traditional long-term care insurance is often called a "use-it-or-lose-it" proposition. Not only that, but you could pay on a traditional long-term care policy for years, only to have the coverage diminished and the rates increased. Notice I use the phrase "traditional" long-term care insurance in describing these policies. That is because new polices exist that have come along in just the last decade or so that offer inventive solutions to this problem. The point is, a competent financial advisor will know about them all and be able to help the client sort through them to see if they are an option.

Bottom line? Selecting the right financial advisor for you may require some action and discernment on your part. The importance of it, however, grows exponentially with the size of your estate and your proximity to the retirement threshold. You are embarking into unfamiliar territory. You want a guide who knows the territory — someone who can help you step safely and confidently as you make your way.

Do they specialize? When you are nearing retirement, your financial advisor must be able to specialize in retirement income planning. A financial plan for someone in their 30s or 40s will be much different from the financial plan of someone in their 60s and 70s. Ask your financial advisor candidate, "Do you specialize in retirement income planning?" Some are great counselors on the accumulation phase of life, but know very little about the preservation and distribution phase. The most critical time window is five to 10 years on either side of retirement. Decisions made in that little window of time will have lasting implications. A financial advisor who specializes in wealth preservation and retirement income planning will be attuned to this and advise you accordingly.

Are they competent with estate planning? Some people confuse estate planning with merely having a will. A bonafide professional will be able to look at your financial picture for retirement and beyond from 30,000 feet up and identify strategies to keep as much of your accumulated wealth in your family name, not Uncle Sam's. Tax traps abound in the transition of wealth from one generation to another.

The "estate tax," or "death tax" as some like to call it, is a moving target. It seems Congress can change the estate tax exemption at will so we won't really know whether we will be affected by it until the time comes. But a competent financial advisor will have the most current understanding of estate taxes and know ways to reduce its effect on clients.

Are they independent? That is not a silly question. Some who hang out a "financial advisor" shingle may work for a company and are limited to that company's financial products. To put it bluntly, they are there to sell you products, not help you plan your financial affairs. It is not illegal for them to do this, but that doesn't make it good for the client. A good financial advisory firm will be independent. Their service will be open-handed and their advice unbiased. The financial advisor you choose to work with should have an entire universe of solutions available, not just a "house menu" from which to choose. This brings us to that word "fiduciary" again.

Make sure your financial advisor has a fiduciary responsibility to you. This makes them legally required and duty bound to act in your best interests apart from any profit motive or self-interest. Aren't all financial advisors obligated to work this way? Not really. Most stockbrokers work for broker-dealers. Essentially, they are there to connect the investor with the investment. They work under the "suitability" standard, which means they are obligated to charge reasonable and appropriate transaction fees and not put the client into any investment that is unsuitable for him or her. That's not the same as the much stricter "fiduciary" standard. The right financial advisory firm for you will most likely have the capability of serving as both a money manager, able to handle transactions involving stocks, bonds, mutual funds, equity traded funds, REITS, etc., and as a qualified financial advisor for financial vehicles provided by such institutions as banks and insurance companies, like CDs and annuities.

No One Size Fits All

Can you imagine buying an expensive pair of shoes without making sure they fit? Of course not! One thing I have learned over the years is that every person is unique, and there is no one-size-fits-all strategy when it comes to helping people achieve their financial goals. If you take two people who are financially identical in every other aspect — same age, same income, same net worth and investments, they will still require different financial plans. They will not share the same goals, desires and dreams. They will not share the same risk tolerance. Their legacy preferences will vary. That is why cookie-cutter solutions offered by some brokerage houses are not workable. Like undersized or oversized shoes, they just don't fit you.

A financial plan, like a tailored suit, will fit you and you will know it. It will clothe you with the appropriate amounts of protection and opportunity you deserve — perfectly tailored to your unique financial circumstances, your wishes, hopes, plans and dreams for the future. The financial advisor who is right for you will know how important that is to you without having to be told.

ABOUT THE AUTHOR

Beth Andrews grew up in South Bend, Indiana, a town situated in the extreme northern end of the state near Lake Michigan. She now lives in the small town of Eighty Four, Pennsylvania, famous for its odd numerical name and for being the headquarters of a national lumber chain by the same name.

After graduating from Indiana University with an accounting degree in 1996, Beth moved right into the financial advisory profession, working with such prestigious corporations as American Express and Ameriprise. She obtained her SEC Series 7 certification in 1997 and began managing portfolios, helping clients invest in stocks, bonds and mutual funds. The 2008 financial crisis had a great impact on Beth's career. After seeing so many retirees lose as much as half their life's savings in the stock market crash, she saw a need for retirees to have safer invest-ment strategies.

"It was a bad time for stockbrokers," Beth remembers. "I could hear the hurt in the voices of some older investors who had lost as much as half of their life's savings when the financial crisis hit. I knew that if I wanted to truly help them I would have to strike out on my own."

Beth started Networth Advisors, a firm with three team members, in 2004. The company's headquarters is in Canonsburg, Pennsylvania, which is near her home. She is an Investment Advisor Representative working with AE Wealth Management LLC, an SEC Registered Investment Advisor. She is a CERTIFIED FINANCIAL PLANNER™ professional, a designation that requires extensive training in taxes, insurance, estate planning and retirement income planning. CFP® professionals are also required to com-plete extensive continuing education courses to maintain their certification. Beth is also a Certified Public Account-ant (CPA) and a Chartered Financial Consultant (ChFC®).

Personal and Family Life

Beth is the daughter of Bill and Gloria Parker, who live in McMurray, Pennsylvania. She has a sister, Lynn, and a brother, Adam.

"My parents have been married for over 50 years," says Beth, who describes her mother as a caring homemaker and "real people person," and her father, an electrical en-gineer, as a numbers-oriented person who pays much attention to detail. "I think I got the best of both of them," she says. "I love making the numbers work for people."

Beth loves horseback riding. She met her husband, Todd, in 1993.   "He was a farrier and was shoeing our horses," explains Beth. "He asked me out for lunch and the rest is history."

"We own paints — the ones with the spots," laughs Beth. "They are well-mannered and excellent mounts. My horse is Jetta and Todd's horse is named CoCo."

Beth and her husband love to take riding vacations. They have been to such faraway places as Australia, Italy and the Grand Canyon. They regularly enjoy riding and camping in large national parks.

Made in the USA
Middletown, DE
11 August 2022

70434802R00086